The Galveston Diet Cookbook

1600 Days of Nourishing, Quick-to-Prepare Recipes for Hormonal Wellness and Weight Mastery. Includes 45 Meal Plan

Elara Belmont

Introduction

Chapter 1: Embarking on the Galveston Journey

Discovering the Galveston Diet

Welcome to the transformative world of the Galveston Diet. As you embark on this journey, it's more than just turning a page in a book; it's about embracing a new chapter in your life. This path is not solely focused on weight loss; it's an enlightening quest towards understanding your body, its hormonal intricacies, and how to nourish it in harmony with your active lifestyle.

At the heart of the Galveston Diet is a deep commitment to hormonal wellness and a balanced lifestyle. It transcends the traditional concept of dieting and evolves into a life choice – a decision to understand and respond to your body's needs with attentiveness and care. This diet is not a one-size-fits-all regimen. It's a personalized approach, meeting you at your unique point in your health journey.

Delving into the science behind the Galveston Diet, we keep it engaging and accessible. Your body is a sophisticated machine, particularly in how it manages hormones. These microscopic messengers significantly influence how you feel, appear, and live your life. The Galveston Diet's foundation lies in the latest scientific insights into hormonal balance and the pivotal role of food in achieving this equilibrium. It's about choosing foods that nurture your hormonal health, not disrupt it.

Designed for the busy individual, the Galveston Diet understands your hectic schedule. Whether you're managing a demanding career, squeezing in Pilates sessions, or exploring the great outdoors, this diet fits seamlessly into your lifestyle. It's for the proactive and curious, those who value mindful, healthful eating but can't afford to spend hours in the kitchen.

The diet introduces you to a world of flavorsome and quick recipes that align with your wellness goals. Imagine vibrant salads assembled in minutes, and delightful smoothies that taste indulgent yet serve as nutritional powerhouses. These recipes cater not just to your health but also to your palate, proving that diet foods can be both nutritious and delicious.

In an ever-evolving landscape of health trends, the Galveston Diet offers a sustainable approach. It stays abreast of the latest dietary trends while rooted in the timeless principles of nutrition. It's not about chasing fleeting fads; it's about understanding and implementing what genuinely benefits your body.

The Galveston Diet serves as your personal wellness guide, navigating you through the complex world of health and nutrition. It's akin to having a friendly expert alongside you, empathizing with the challenges of balancing a hectic life with the desire to eat well. This book is not just a compilation of recipes; it's a companion in your journey towards wellness.

Crafted with a blend of humor, empathy, and authoritative, science-backed information, the Galveston Diet understands your struggles - finding time for nutritious meals, keeping up with health trends, and dealing with conflicting dietary advice. It offers practical solutions to these challenges, making your journey towards better health an enjoyable and fulfilling experience.

As you delve into the Galveston Diet, remember that this is more than a dietary change. It's a journey of discovery towards a more balanced, energized, and harmonious life. Welcome to a world where each meal is a step towards a healthier, happier you.

The Science of Hormonal Wellness

At the essence of the Galveston Diet is a philosophy that intersects cutting-edge scientific research with practical, everyday sensibility. It's a diet that speaks directly to the body's hormonal needs, addressing them with carefully chosen, nourishing foods that delight the palate. Designed for real people who juggle careers, hobbies, and social lives, the Galveston Diet is for the graphic designer who finds solace in Pilates, for the busy professional seeking quick, nutritious meals, and for the wellness enthusiast who spends her leisure time reading and attending health retreats.

The foundation of this diet is built on the latest scientific understanding of hormonal balance and its profound impact on overall health and weight management. It transcends the fad diets that come and go, focusing instead on the crucial role hormones play in our wellbeing. The Galveston Diet demystifies the science of hormones in an engaging and relatable way, making it not just informative but also an enjoyable read.

Recognizing the challenges of a busy schedule, the Galveston Diet is designed to integrate seamlessly into your lifestyle. It offers quick, nutritious recipes that cater to a range of needs - whether you're looking for a post-workout smoothie or a healthy meal to fuel a busy day. Time is a precious commodity, and this diet emphasizes efficiency without compromising on nutritional value.

A cornerstone of the Galveston Diet is its emphasis on culinary enjoyment. It dispels the notion that healthy eating must be bland, introducing a variety of recipes that are as delicious as they are nutritious. From energizing breakfasts to satisfying dinners, each recipe is a celebration of flavors, colors, and textures, proving that healthy eat

Part I: Foundations of the Galveston Diet

Chapter 2: The Pillars of Hormonal Balance

Understanding Your Body

Embarking on the journey of the Galveston Diet, it's essential to start with a fundamental step: understanding your body. This understanding is crucial, not just in the context of weight management or health, but as an integral part of your overall well-being. Your body is not just a physical entity; it's a complex system where every part works in harmony, influenced significantly by hormones. In Chapter 2, "The Pillars of Hormonal Balance," we delve deep into the importance of understanding your body, particularly how hormones affect your health, mood, and metabolism.

Your body communicates with you in various ways, often through signals that are easy to overlook in the hustle of daily life. Whether it's the energy dip after lunch or the mood swings that seem inexplicable, these are your body's ways of telling you something. Understanding these signals is the first step towards achieving hormonal balance. Hormones like insulin, cortisol, estrogen, and thyroid hormones, to name a few, play a pivotal role in regulating various bodily functions. The balance of these hormones is crucial for maintaining optimal health.

In today's fast-paced lifestyle, where activities like Pilates, hiking, and experimenting with healthy recipes are often interspersed with attending wellness retreats and consuming digital content, it's easy to lose touch with our body's natural rhythm. This disconnect can lead to imbalances that manifest in various forms - weight gain, fatigue, stress, and other health issues. The Galveston Diet is designed to help you reconnect with your body, understanding its needs, and responding in ways that promote hormonal balance.

This chapter is not just about the science of hormones; it's about making that science accessible and relatable. Through engaging, scientifically grounded discussions, we explore how different aspects of your lifestyle - from the food you eat to the way you manage stress - can impact your hormonal health. It's about empowering you with knowledge and practical tools to make informed choices about your diet and lifestyle.

Understanding your body also means recognizing its uniqueness. What works for one person may not work for another. This is why the Galveston Diet emphasizes a personalized approach. It encourages you to listen to your body, understand its unique language, and respond with care and attention. This approach is not about following a rigid set of rules; it's about adapting principles to fit your individual needs and lifestyle.

As you journey through this chapter, you'll gain insights into how to harmonize your lifestyle with your body's needs. It's about creating a balance that goes beyond the plate - encompassing your mental, emotional, and physical health. Whether you're a busy professional, a health enthusiast, or someone just starting their wellness journey, understanding your body is the first step towards a healthier, more balanced you.

In conclusion, "Understanding Your Body" is a chapter that goes to the heart of the Galveston Diet. It lays the foundation for a journey that's not just about eating right but living right. It's an invitation to start a conversation with your body, to learn its language, and to respond with love and care. As you turn these pages, you embark on a path of discovery, empowerment, and above all, balance. Welcome to a journey where understanding your body is the key to unlocking a healthier, happier you.

Key Nutrients for Hormonal Health

In the journey of discovering the Galveston Diet, a pivotal aspect is understanding the key nutrients essential for hormonal health. This understanding isn't just about knowing what to eat; it's about recognizing how these nutrients interact with your body, particularly your hormonal system, to promote a balanced, healthy lifestyle. In the second chapter of "The Pillars of Hormonal Balance," we explore these nutrients in depth, weaving a tapestry of dietary wisdom that aligns with the latest health trends and fits into the busy lifestyle of a proactive, wellness-oriented individual.

Hormones, the chemical messengers in our body, play a crucial role in regulating numerous physiological processes. Their balance is essential for our overall well-being. However, in today's fast-paced world, maintaining this balance can be challenging. Factors such as stress, lack of sleep, and, most importantly, our diet, significantly impact our hormonal health. This is where the Galveston Diet steps in, introducing a holistic approach to eating that nourishes not just the body but also the hormonal system.

Healthy Fats: The Foundation of Hormonal Health

Healthy fats are often misunderstood. However, in the realm of hormonal health, they are foundational. Hormones are synthesized from fats, making fats an essential component of a hormone-friendly diet. Sources of healthy fats like avocados, nuts, seeds, and olive oil play a significant role in the Galveston Diet. These facts are not just sources of energy; they are building blocks for your hormones. They help in the production of hormones and reduce inflammation, a key disruptor of hormonal balance.

Proteins: Building Blocks for Hormonal Health

Proteins are another cornerstone of hormonal health. They provide essential amino acids, the building blocks for hormone synthesis. For individuals who enjoy an active lifestyle, with hobbies like Pilates and hiking, adequate protein intake is crucial. It supports muscle recovery, energy levels, and hormone production. The Galveston Diet emphasizes the importance of high-quality protein sources, such as lean meats, fish, legumes, and dairy products, ensuring that each meal contributes to hormonal harmony.

Fiber: Regulating Hormones Naturally

Fiber plays a dual role in hormonal balance. It aids in digestion and helps regulate blood sugar levels, which, in turn, supports hormonal equilibrium. A diet rich in high-fiber foods such as vegetables, fruits, and whole grains is a key component of the Galveston Diet. These foods not only keep the digestive system running smoothly but also help maintain consistent energy levels and mood.

Antioxidants: Protecting Hormonal Health

Antioxidants combat oxidative stress, which can disrupt hormonal balance. The Galveston Diet includes a variety of antioxidant-rich foods like berries, leafy greens, and even dark chocolate. These foods protect the body against oxidative stress, promoting overall hormonal health.

Micronutrients: The Fine-Tuners of Hormonal Health

Vitamins and minerals play specific roles in hormonal health. Micronutrients such as vitamin D, magnesium, and zinc are vital for the production, regulation, and function of hormones. The Galveston Diet not only highlights the importance of these nutrients but also guides you on how to incorporate them into your meals. Whether it's through a sun-kissed morning walk for vitamin D or a magnesium-rich snack of almonds and pumpkin seeds, these micronutrients are seamlessly integrated into your diet.

Aligning Recipes with Dietary Goals

The recipes in the Galveston Diet are meticulously crafted to align with its hormonal health principles. If the diet's focus is on low-carb eating, the recipes reflect this, ensuring that each meal contributes to your hormonal balance and dietary goals. It's not just about what you eat; it's about ensuring that what you eat serves your body's needs.

Customization: Tailoring to Individual Needs

Understanding that each body is unique, the Galveston Diet encourages customization. It empowers you to tailor your diet according to your individual hormonal health needs, lifestyle, and preferences. Whether you're experimenting with healthy recipes or seeking quick, nutritious meals, the diet adapts to you, not the other way around.

A Diet that Fits Your Lifestyle

The Galveston Diet isn't just a list of foods; it's a lifestyle. It fits into your busy schedule, aligning with your hobbies and activities. Whether you're attending a wellness retreat or scrolling through health blogs, the diet offers practical, delicious, and hormone-balancing meal options.

In summary, "Key Nutrients for Hormonal Health" in the Galveston Diet is more than a dietary guideline; it's a comprehensive approach to eating that nurtures your hormonal health. It understands the challenges of a busy lifestyle and the need to stay updated with the latest health trends. By focusing on healthy fats, proteins, fiber, antioxidants, and micronutrients, and aligning recipes with these dietary goals, the Galveston Diet offers a sustainable, enjoyable path to hormonal balance and overall wellness.

The Role of Diet in Weight Mastery

In the pursuit of weight mastery, the role of diet is both intricate and profound. The journey is not just about the scales tipping in your favor; it's about understanding and harnessing the power of food to create a harmonious relationship between your body and your lifestyle. Within the pages of "The Galveston Diet Cookbook for Beginners," the concept of weight mastery is redefined. It's seen not as a fleeting goal but as a sustainable, enjoyable lifestyle, deeply rooted in the understanding of how diet influences every aspect of our well-being.

Weight Mastery: More Than Just Calories

Traditionally, weight loss has been simplified to a game of numbers – calories in versus calories out. However, this approach overlooks the complexity of the human body, particularly the role of hormones in weight regulation. The Galveston Diet introduces a more nuanced perspective, emphasizing that it's not just about the quantity of what we eat, but the quality and composition of our diet that truly matters.

Understanding the Hormonal Impact on Weight
Hormones like insulin, cortisol, and leptin play pivotal roles in weight management. For instance, insulin, the hormone responsible for glucose regulation, can also dictate how our body stores fat. An imbalanced diet can lead to insulin resistance, a key factor in weight gain and difficulty in losing weight. The Galveston Diet focuses on foods that maintain healthy insulin levels, combining low-glycemic carbohydrates, healthy fats, and lean proteins to achieve hormonal balance.

The Role of Macronutrients in Weight Mastery
Each macronutrient – carbohydrates, fats, and proteins – plays a specific role in weight management. Carbohydrates, when consumed in their whole, unprocessed form, provide essential energy without spiking blood sugar levels. Healthy fats, once misunderstood, are now celebrated for their ability to satiate and provide sustained energy. Proteins are crucial for building and maintaining muscle mass, which in turn helps in burning calories efficiently.

Fiber: The Unsung Hero of Weight Management
Fiber is a critical component of the Galveston Diet. It not only aids in digestion but also helps in feeling fuller for longer periods. High-fiber foods, such as vegetables and whole grains, play a significant role in weight control. They work by slowing down digestion, stabilizing blood sugar levels, and preventing overeating.

Microbiome and Weight Mastery
Recent research underscores the role of the gut microbiome in weight management. A diet rich in varied, nutrient-dense foods promotes a healthy gut, which in turn can positively impact weight control. The Galveston Diet includes a diverse range of foods that nourish the gut microbiome, supporting overall health and aiding in weight management.

Aligning Recipes with Diet Goals
The recipes in the Galveston Diet are carefully crafted to align with the principles of hormonal balance and weight mastery. Each recipe is a blend of taste and nutrition, ensuring that the meals are enjoyable and in sync with weight management goals. Whether the focus is on low-carb, high-protein, or rich in healthy fats, the recipes cater to a range of dietary needs while keeping weight mastery in sight.

Lifestyle Integration: Making Diet a Natural Part of Life
Integrating dietary changes into one's lifestyle can be challenging, especially for those with a busy schedule. The Galveston Diet addresses this challenge by offering recipes and meal ideas that are not only healthy but also quick and easy to prepare. The diet encourages experimentation with healthy recipes, aligning with hobbies and activities like Pilates, hiking, or attending wellness retreats. It's designed to fit seamlessly into a busy lifestyle, making weight mastery a natural and enjoyable part of everyday life.

Chapter 3: Setting Up for Success

Stocking Your Galveston Kitchen

Stocking Your Galveston Kitchen" is a pivotal chapter in the Galveston Diet journey, encapsulating the essence of setting yourself up for success. It's not just about filling your pantry and refrigerator with food; it's about creating a sanctuary that supports your dietary goals and complements your lifestyle. This chapter isn't just a guide; it's the foundation of your journey towards a balanced, healthy lifestyle, aligning with the latest health trends and fitting seamlessly into your busy schedule.

Creating a Kitchen that Reflects Your Health Goals
The first step in stocking your Galveston kitchen is to create an environment that reflects your health goals. This means a kitchen where every item, every ingredient, serves a purpose towards your wellness. It's about making your kitchen a place of inspiration and positivity, a space where healthy eating is not just easy but also enjoyable.

Essentials for a Galveston Kitchen
A well-stocked Galveston kitchen is rich in whole, unprocessed foods. Think fresh vegetables and fruits, whole grains, lean proteins, healthy fats, and herbs and spices. These are the building blocks of the Galveston Diet, ingredients that not only nourish your body but also bring joy and creativity to your cooking.

Vegetables and Fruits: The Cornerstones of Nutrition
Vegetables and fruits are the cornerstones of the Galveston Diet. They are rich in vitamins, minerals, fiber, and antioxidants, making them essential for hormonal balance and overall health. Stocking a variety of colors and types ensures that you get a broad spectrum of nutrients. Think leafy greens, berries, citrus fruits, and cruciferous vegetables like broccoli and cauliflower.

Whole Grains: Sustained Energy and Fiber
Whole grains like quinoa, brown rice, and oats are staples in the Galveston kitchen. They provide sustained energy and are rich in fiber, which is crucial for digestive health and maintaining a feeling of fullness. These grains can be the base for a variety of meals, from breakfast porridges to hearty dinner bowls.

Lean Proteins: Building and Repairing Tissues

Proteins are essential for building and repairing tissues. They are also crucial for hormone production. Lean protein sources like chicken, fish, eggs, and plant-based options like legumes and tofu should have a permanent place in your Galveston kitchen. They can be easily incorporated into meals, ensuring that your protein needs are met throughout the day.

Healthy Fats: Essential for Hormonal Health

Healthy fats are vital for hormonal health. They help in the absorption of vitamins and provide essential fatty acids that the body cannot produce on its own. Stocking your kitchen with sources of healthy fats like avocados, nuts, seeds, and olive oil is essential for the Galveston Diet. These fats not only add flavor to your meals but also contribute to your overall health.

Herbs and Spices: Flavor Without the Calories

Herbs and spices are the secret weapons in your Galveston kitchen. They add flavor without adding extra calories. Fresh herbs like basil, cilantro, and parsley, and spices like turmeric, cinnamon, and ginger, can transform a simple dish into a culinary masterpiece. They also come with their own health benefits, from anti-inflammatory properties to digestive aids.

Beverages: Hydration and Health

Hydration is key in the Galveston Diet. Water should be your primary beverage, but herbal teas and infused waters with fruits and herbs can also be included for variety. These beverages keep you hydrated, aid in digestion, and can be a calming ritual in your daily routine.

Tools for Success: Equipping Your Kitchen

Having the right tools in your kitchen can make meal preparation easier and more enjoyable. A good set of knives, a blender for smoothies and soups, and a variety of pots and pans are essential. Meal prep containers for storing leftovers or prepping meals in advance can also be helpful, especially for those with a busy schedule.

Mindful Shopping: Aligning Purchases with Goals

Stocking your Galveston kitchen starts with mindful shopping. It means choosing ingredients that align with the dietary principles of the Galveston Diet, like low-carb or high-protein, depending on your focus. It's about being proactive and curious, exploring new foods and ingredients that support your health goals.

In conclusion, "Stocking Your Galveston Kitchen" is more than just a chapter; it's a blueprint for success. It guides you in creating a kitchen that supports your journey towards a balanced, healthy lifestyle. By aligning your kitchen with your diet goals, you set the stage for success, making healthy eating a natural, enjoyable part of your daily life.

Navigating Grocery Shopping

Navigating the aisles of a grocery store can be a daunting task, especially when adopting a new dietary lifestyle like the Galveston Diet. It's not just about picking up food items; it's about making informed choices that align with your health goals. In "Navigating Grocery Shopping," a critical section of Chapter 3 in "Setting Up for Success," we delve deep into how to make grocery shopping a seamless, efficient, and even enjoyable part of your journey towards a balanced and healthy lifestyle.

Transforming Grocery Shopping from Chore to Adventure
Grocery shopping can feel like a mundane task, but with the Galveston Diet, it transforms into an adventure of discovering new ingredients and flavors. It's about exploring the grocery store with curiosity and open-mindedness, choosing foods that not only tantalize your taste buds but also nourish your body.

Strategic Planning: The Key to Efficient Shopping
Before heading to the store, planning is crucial. It involves understanding what ingredients are needed to create the delicious, health-focused recipes from the Galveston Diet Cookbook. This planning doesn't just save time; it ensures that your shopping aligns with your dietary principles, whether it's low-carb, high-protein, or rich in healthy fats.

Understanding Food Labels: Beyond the Marketing Hype
One of the essential skills in grocery shopping is understanding food labels. It's easy to get swayed by marketing claims like "low-fat" or "natural," but the Galveston Diet teaches you to look beyond these claims. It's about examining the ingredients list and nutritional information to make choices that are truly beneficial for your health.

Choosing Fresh and Whole Foods
The foundation of the Galveston Diet is fresh, whole foods. This means prioritizing the perimeter of the grocery store where fresh produce, meats, and dairy are typically located. It's about filling your cart with a rainbow of vegetables and fruits, lean proteins, and whole grains that are the cornerstone of a hormone-balancing, nutritious diet.

The Importance of Quality in Proteins and Fats
When selecting proteins and fats, quality is key. This means choosing grass-fed meats, free-range poultry, wild-caught fish, and organic, pasture-raised eggs. For fats, opting for unprocessed options like extra virgin olive oil, avocados, nuts, and seeds. These choices not only provide superior nutrition but also align with the principles of sustainable, healthy eating.

Incorporating Variety for Nutritional Balance
Variety is not just the spice of life; it's also crucial for nutritional balance. This means experimenting with different types of grains, a variety of protein sources, and diverse fruits and vegetables. Each offers unique nutrients and benefits, contributing to a well-rounded diet.

Mindful of Allergies and Dietary Restrictions
The Galveston Diet acknowledges that individual dietary needs vary, including allergies and sensitivities. It advises on how to navigate these challenges, choosing substitutes that align with the diet's principles without compromising on taste or nutrition.

Seasonal Shopping: Aligning Diet with Nature
Shopping seasonally is another aspect emphasized in the Galveston Diet. It means choosing fruits and vegetables that are in season, not only for their peak flavor and nutrition but also for their environmental benefits. Seasonal shopping often aligns with local produce, supporting community farmers and reducing the carbon footprint.

Budget-Friendly Tips for Healthy Eating
Eating healthy doesn't have to break the bank. The Galveston Diet provides tips on how to shop smartly, such as buying in bulk, choosing store brands for basic ingredients, and being mindful of sales and discounts. It's about making the diet accessible and sustainable, regardless of your budget.

Staying Informed and Inspired
Staying informed and inspired is crucial for successful grocery shopping. This means staying updated with the latest health trends through podcasts, influencers, and health food expos. It also involves seeking inspiration for new recipes and ingredients, keeping your diet diverse and enjoyable.

In conclusion, "Navigating Grocery Shopping" in the Galveston Diet is more than just a guide to buying food. It's a comprehensive approach to selecting ingredients that support your health goals, fit into your lifestyle, and bring joy to your cooking. It's about making informed, mindful choices that transform grocery shopping from a chore into a delightful adventure in your journey towards a balanced, healthy lifestyle.

Time-Saving Cooking Techniques

In the bustling rhythm of modern life, finding time to prepare nutritious meals can be a significant challenge, especially for those committed to maintaining a balanced, healthy lifestyle. The Galveston Diet recognizes this challenge and addresses it head-on in the chapter titled "Time-Saving Cooking Techniques." This section is not just a compilation of quick recipes; it's a comprehensive guide to revolutionizing your cooking methods to align with your busy schedule, dietary goals, and wellness aspirations.

Embracing Efficiency in the Kitchen

The art of time-saving cooking begins with embracing efficiency in the kitchen. It's about transforming your approach to meal preparation, making it a streamlined, stress-free experience. This involves smart planning, organizing your workspace, and adopting cooking techniques that save time without compromising the nutritional value or taste of your food.

Planning: The Cornerstone of Quick Cooking

Strategic meal planning is a critical aspect of the Galveston Diet. It involves mapping out your meals for the week, considering your schedule, dietary needs, and personal preferences. This planning doesn't just save time; it also ensures that your meals align with the Galveston Diet's principles, whether focusing on low-carb, high-protein, or rich in healthy fats. It's about making informed choices, shopping efficiently, and avoiding last-minute decisions that often lead to less healthy options.

Prep Once, Eat Multiple Times

A game-changer in saving time is the concept of batch cooking or preparing multiple portions of a meal in one go. This approach is particularly useful for components that take longer to cook, like grains, proteins, or roasted vegetables. By cooking in larger quantities, you have ready-to-use ingredients that can be quickly assembled into various meals throughout the week.

Utilizing Kitchen Gadgets and Tools

Modern kitchen gadgets and tools are allies in your time-saving quest. Devices like slow cookers, pressure cookers, and blenders can be invaluable. They allow for hands-off cooking, where the meal prepares itself while you attend to other tasks. For instance, a slow cooker can simmer a stew to perfection without your constant supervision, while a blender can whip up a nutritious smoothie in seconds.

The Magic of One-Pot Meals

One-pot meals are a cornerstone of efficient cooking. They minimize both cooking time and cleanup. These meals, which include stews, casseroles, and stir-fries, are not just time savers; they're also perfect for combining a variety of ingredients to create a balanced, flavorful dish that aligns with your dietary goals.

Quick-Cooking Ingredients: Your Go-To Allies

Incorporating quick-cooking ingredients is another effective strategy. Foods like quinoa, couscous, or certain types of pasta cook in a fraction of the time compared to their more time-consuming counterparts. Combining these with fresh or pre-chopped vegetables and a protein source can result in a nutritious, delicious meal in no time.

The Freezer: Your Time-Saving Friend

The freezer is an often-underutilized resource in time-saving cooking. Freezing portions of prepared meals, sauces, or prepped ingredients can be a lifesaver on particularly busy days. It's about having a backup plan that aligns with your diet and saves you from resorting to less healthy, convenient options.

Making the Most of Leftovers

Transforming leftovers into new meals is an art form in the Galveston Diet. It's about looking at leftovers not as mere repeats but as bases for new culinary creations. A roasted chicken from dinner can become the next day's salad topping or a filling for a wrap, offering variety without additional cooking time.

Cooking Techniques That Retain Nutritional Value

The Galveston Diet emphasizes cooking techniques that retain the nutritional value of food. Methods like steaming, quick sautéing, or grilling are not just quick but also help in preserving the vitamins and minerals in your ingredients. It's about making every minute in the kitchen count, both in terms of time and nutritional value.

Staying Informed and Inspired

Staying informed and inspired is key to keeping your cooking techniques aligned with your health goals. This means keeping up with the latest culinary trends through podcasts, blogs, and influencers. It's about continuous learning and adapting, ensuring that your cooking methods evolve with your dietary needs and preferences.

Part II: Recipe Chapters

Chapter4: Morning Energizers

Energizing Smoothies

Recipe 1: Almond Flour Blueberry Pancakes

Preparation Time: 15 minutes

Ingredients:
- Almond Flour: 1 cup
- Fresh Blueberries: 1/2 cup
- Egg: 1 large
- Unsweetened Almond Milk: 1/2 cup
- Baking Powder: 1 tsp
- Vanilla Extract: 1 tsp
- Coconut Oil (for cooking): 2 tbsp

Method of Cooking: Pan-frying

Procedure:

1. Mix almond flour, baking powder in a bowl.
2. Whisk in the egg, almond milk, and vanilla extract.
3. Gently fold in blueberries.
4. Heat coconut oil in a pan, pour batter to form pancakes.
5. Cook until golden brown on both sides.

Nutritional Values: Calories: 280 per serving

Servings: Makes 2 servings

Recipe 2: Chia Seed Yogurt Parfait

Preparation Time:
10 minutes (plus overnight soaking)
Ingredients:
- Chia Seeds: 3 tbsp
- Greek Yogurt: 1 cup
- Honey: 1 tbsp
- Mixed Berries: 1/2 cup
- Almonds (slivered): 2 tbsp

Method of Cooking:
No-cook, refrigeration

Procedure:
1. Soak chia seeds in water overnight.
2. Layer Greek yogurt, soaked chia seeds, honey, and berries in a glass.
3. Top with slivered almonds.

Nutritional Values:
Calories: 350 per serving
Servings:
Makes 1 serving

Recipe 3: Spinach and Feta Omelets

Preparation Time:
10 minutes
Ingredients:
- Eggs: 2 large
- Fresh Spinach: 1 cup
- Feta Cheese (crumbled): 1/4 cup
- Olive Oil: 1 tsp
- Salt and Pepper: To taste

Method of Cooking:
Pan-frying
Procedure:

1. Beat eggs, salt, and pepper in a bowl.
2. Sauté spinach in olive oil until wilted.
3. Pour eggs over spinach, sprinkle feta on top.
4. Fold omelet, cook until eggs are set.

Nutritional Values:
Calories: 320 per serving
Servings:
Makes 1 serving

Recipe 4: Avocado Toast with Poached Egg

Preparation Time:
15 minutes
Ingredients:
- Whole Grain Bread: 1 slice
- Avocado: 1/2, mashed
- Egg: 1 large
- Olive Oil: 1 tsp
- Salt and Pepper: To taste
- Red Pepper Flakes: A pinch

Method of Cooking:
Poaching, toasting

Procedure:
1. Poach the egg.
2. Toast the bread slice.
3. Spread mashed avocado on toast.
4. Top with poached egg, season with salt, pepper, and red pepper flakes.

Nutritional Values: Calories: 300 per serving
Servings: Makes 1 serving

Recipe 5: Overnight Oats with Almond Butter

Preparation Time:
5 minutes (plus overnight refrigeration)

Ingredients:
- Rolled Oats: 1/2 cup
- Almond Milk: 1/2 cup
- Almond Butter: 1 tbsp
- Maple Syrup: 1 tsp
- Chopped Nuts: 1 tbsp

Method of Cooking:
No-cook, refrigeration

Procedure:

1. Combine oats and almond milk in a jar.
2. Stir in almond butter and maple syrup.
3. Refrigerate overnight.
4. Top with chopped nuts before serving.

Nutritional Values:
Calories: 350 per serving
Servings:
Makes 1 serving

Recipe 7: Protein-Packed Quinoa Bowl

Preparation Time:
20 minutes

Ingredients:
- Quinoa (cooked): 1 cup
- Hard-Boiled Egg: 1
- Avocado (sliced): 1/2
- Cherry Tomatoes (halved): 1/2 cup
- Olive Oil: 1 tsp
- Lemon Juice: 1 tbsp
- Salt and Pepper: To taste

Method of Cooking:
Boiling

Procedure:

1. Cook quinoa as per instructions.
2. Slice hard-boiled egg and avocado.
3. Combine quinoa, egg, avocado, and tomatoes in a bowl.
4. Drizzle with olive oil and lemon juice, season with salt and pepper.

Nutritional Values:
Calories: 450 per serving
Servings:
Makes 1 serving

Recipe 8: Berry and Nut Butter Smoothie

Preparation Time: 5 minutes

Ingredients:
- Mixed Berries (frozen): 1 cup
- Almond Butter: 1 tbsp
- Greek Yogurt: 1/2 cup
- Almond Milk: 1/2cup
- Honey: 1 tsp

Method of Cooking: Blending

Procedure:

1. Combine all ingredients in a blender.
2. Blend until smooth.

Nutritional Values:
Calories: 300 per serving
Servings: Makes 1 serving

Recipe 9: Turkey Bacon and Avocado Wrap

Preparation Time:
10 minutes
Ingredients:
- Whole Grain Tortilla: 1
- Turkey Bacon (cooked): 2 strips
- Avocado (sliced): 1/2
- Lettuce: 1/2 cup
- Tomato (sliced): 1/2
- Mustard: 1 tsp

Method of Cooking:
Pan-frying (for bacon)

Procedure:
1. Cook turkey bacon until crispy.
2. Lay tortilla flat, layer lettuce, tomato, avocado, and bacon.
3. Drizzle with mustard, roll into a wrap.

Nutritional Values:
Calories: 350 per serving
Servings:
Makes 1 serving

Recipe 10: Greek Yogurt with Honey and Walnuts

Preparation Time:
5 minutes
Ingredients:
- Greek Yogurt: 1 cup
- Honey: 1 tbsp
- Walnuts (chopped): 2 tbsp

Method of Cooking:
No-cook, assembling

Procedure:
1. Scoop Greek yogurt into a bowl.
1. Drizzle with honey and top with chopped walnuts.

Nutritional Values:
Calories: 300 per serving
Servings:
Makes   1   serving

Quick Breakfasts

Recipe 1: Mediterranean Frittata Muffins

Preparation Time: 20 minutes
Ingredients:
- Eggs: 6 large
- Spinach: 1 cup, chopped
- Feta Cheese: 1/3 cup, crumbled
- Cherry Tomatoes: 1/2 cup, halved
- Olive Oil: 1 tbsp
- Salt and Pepper: To taste

Method of Cooking: Baking

Procedure: Preheat oven to 375°F (190°C). Grease muffin tin with olive oil.
1. Beat eggs in a bowl, season with salt and pepper.
2. Stir in spinach, feta cheese, and tomatoes.
3. Pour mixture into muffin tin, bake for 15 minutes.

Nutritional Values: Calories: 120

Recipe 2: Tropical Coconut Chia Pudding

Preparation Time:
15 minutes (plus overnight refrigeration)

Ingredients:
- Chia Seeds: 1/4 cup
- Coconut Milk: 1 cup
- Pineapple (diced): 1/2 cup
- Shredded Coconut: 2 tbsp
- Honey: 1 tbsp

Method of Cooking:
Refrigeration

Procedure:
1. Mix chia seeds with coconut milk and honey.
2. Refrigerate overnight until set.
3. Top with diced pineapple and shredded coconut.

Nutritional Values:
Calories: 300 per serving

Servings:
Makes 2 servings

Recipe 3: Savory Quinoa Breakfast Bowl

Preparation Time:
30 minutes

Ingredients:
- Quinoa: 1 cup
- Avocado: 1, sliced
- Cherry Tomatoes: 1/2 cup, halved
- Kale: 1 cup, chopped
- Lemon Juice: 2 tbsp
- Olive Oil: 1 tbsp
- Salt and Pepper: To taste

Method of Cooking:
Boiling, sautéing

Procedure:
1. Cook quinoa as per package instructions.
2. Sauté kale in olive oil until wilted.
3. Combine quinoa, kale, tomatoes, and avocado in a bowl.
4. Drizzle with lemon juice, season with salt and pepper.

Nutritional Values:
Calories: 400 per serving

Servings:
Makes 2 servings

Recipe 4: Protein Power Smoothie

Preparation Time:
5 minutes

Ingredients:
- Spinach: 1 cup
- Greek Yogurt: 1/2 cup
- Almond Milk: 1 cup
- Banana: 1
- Peanut Butter: 1 tbsp
- Honey: 1 tsp

Method of Cooking:
Blending

Procedure:
1. Combine all ingredients in a blender.
1. Blend until smooth.

Nutritional Values:
Calories: 350 per serving

Servings: Makes 1 serving

Recipe 5: Avocado and Egg Breakfast Toast

Preparation Time:
10 minutes
Ingredients:
- Whole Grain Bread: 2 slices
- Avocado: 1, mashed
- Eggs: 2, poached
- Olive Oil: 1 tsp
- Salt and Pepper: To taste
- Red Pepper Flakes: A pinch

Method of Cooking:
Poaching, toasting
Procedure:

1. Poach eggs.
2. Toast bread, spread mashed avocado.
3. Top each toast with a poached egg.
4. Drizzle with olive oil, season with salt, pepper, and red pepper flakes.

Nutritional Values:
Calories: 400 per serving
Servings:
Makes 2 servings

Recipe 6: Greek Yogurt with Mixed Berries and Nuts

Preparation Time:
5 minutes
Ingredients:
- Greek Yogurt: 1 cup
- Mixed Berries: 1/2 cup
- Mixed Nuts (chopped): 1/4 cup
- Honey: 1 tbsp

Method of Cooking:
Assembling

Procedure:

1. Scoop Greek yogurt into a bowl.
2. Top with mixed berries and nuts.
3. Drizzle with honey.

Nutritional Values:
Calories: 350 per serving
Servings:
Makes 1 serving

Recipe 7: Scrambled Tofu with Spinach and Tomatoes

Preparation Time:
15 minutes
Ingredients:
- Firm Tofu: 1 block, crumbled
- Spinach: 1 cup
- Cherry Tomatoes: 1/2 cup, halved
- Turmeric: 1 tsp
- Olive Oil: 1 tbsp
- Salt and Pepper: To taste

Method of Cooking:
Sautéing
Procedure:

1. Heat olive oil in a pan.
2. Add crumbled tofu, turmeric, salt, and pepper.
3. Sauté until slightly golden.
4. Stir in spinach and tomatoes, cook until spinach is wilted.

Nutritional Values:
Calories: 250 per serving
Servings: Makes 2 servings

Recipe 8: Oatmeal with Cinnamon and Apples

Preparation Time:
15 minutes

Ingredients:
- Rolled Oats: 1 cup
- Almond Milk: 2 cups
- Apple: 1, diced
- Cinnamon: 1 tsp
- Honey: 1 tbsp
- Walnuts: 2 tbsp, chopped

Method of Cooking:
Boiling

Procedure:
1. Cook oats in almond milk until soft.
2. Stir in cinnamon and honey.
3. Top with diced apple and chopped walnuts.

Nutritional Values:
Calories: 350 per serving

Servings:
Makes 2 servings

Recipe 9: Veggie Breakfast Burrito

Preparation Time:
20 minutes

Ingredients:
- Whole Wheat Tortilla: 2
- Eggs: 4, beaten
- Bell Pepper: 1, diced
- Onion: 1/2, diced
- Spinach: 1 cup
- Cheddar Cheese: 1/4 cup, shredded
- Salsa: 2 tbsp
- Olive Oil: 1 tbsp
- Salt and Pepper: To taste

Method of Cooking:
Sautéing, assembling

Procedure:
1. Sauté bell pepper and onion in olive oil.
2. Add beaten eggs, cook until scrambled.
3. Stir in spinach until wilted.
4. Divide mixture onto tortillas, top with cheese and salsa.
5. Roll into burritos.

Nutritional Values:
Calories: 400 per burrito

Servings:
Makes 2 burritos

Recipe 10: Banana Nut Muffins

Preparation Time:
30 minutes

Ingredients:
Whole Wheat Flour: 1 1/2 cups
- Ripe Bananas: 3, mashed
- Honey: 1/2 cup
- Egg: 1
- Baking Soda: 1 tsp
- Vanilla Extract: 1 tsp
- Walnuts: 1/2 cup, chopped
- Cinnamon: 1/2 tsp

Method of Cooking:
Baking

Procedure:
1. Preheat oven to 350°F (175°C).

1. Mix flour, baking soda, and cinnamon.
2. In another bowl, combine bananas, honey, egg, and vanilla.
3. Mix dry and wet ingredients, fold in walnuts.
4. Pour into muffin tins, bake for 20 minutes.

Nutritional Values:
Calories: 200 per muffin
Servings:
Makes 12 muffins

Recipe 11: Berry Quinoa Breakfast Salad

Preparation Time:
20 minutes
Ingredients:
- Quinoa (cooked): 1 cup
- Mixed Berries: 1 cup
- Greek Yogurt: 1/2 cup
- Honey: 1 tbsp
- Almonds: 1/4 cup, slivered
- Mint Leaves: A few, for garnish

Method of Cooking:
Assembling
Procedure:

1. Combine cooked quinoa and berries in a bowl.
2. Top with Greek yogurt and almonds.
3. Drizzle with honey, garnish with mint leaves.

Nutritional Values:
Calories: 350 per serving
Servings:
Makes 2 servings

Weekend Brunch Favorites

Recipe 1: Zesty Avocado and Egg Breakfast Tacos

Preparation Time:
20 minutes
Ingredients:
- Whole Wheat Tortillas: 4
- Eggs: 4, scrambled
- Avocado: 2, mashed
- Cherry Tomatoes: 1/2 cup, diced
- Red Onion: 1/4 cup, finely chopped
- Lime Juice: 2 tbsp
- Cilantro: 1/4 cup, chopped
- Olive Oil: 1 tbsp
- Salt and Pepper: To taste

Method of Cooking:
Scrambling, assembling
Procedure:
1. Scramble eggs in olive oil, season with salt and pepper.
2. Mix avocado, lime juice, salt, and pepper.
3. Warm tortillas, spread mashed avocado.
4. Top with scrambled eggs, tomatoes, onion, and cilantro.

Nutritional Values:
Calories: 300 per taco
Servings:
Makes 4 tacos

Recipe 2: Spinach and Mushroom Frittata

Preparation Time: 30 minutes
Ingredients:
- Eggs: 6, beaten
- Fresh Spinach: 2 cups
- Mushrooms: 1 cup, sliced
- Feta Cheese: 1/2 cup, crumbled
- Olive Oil: 1 tbsp
- Salt and Pepper: To taste

Method of Cooking: Baking
Procedure:
1. Preheat oven to 375°F (190°C).
2. Sauté mushrooms and spinach in olive oil.
3. Mix eggs, feta, salt, and pepper.
4. Combine with sautéed veggies, pour into baking dish.
5. Bake for 20 minutes.

Nutritional Values:
Calories: 200 per serving
Servings:
Makes 6 servings

Recipe 3: Almond Flour Banana Bread

Preparation Time:
60 minutes
Ingredients:
- Almond Flour: 2 cups
- Ripe Bananas: 3, mashed
- Eggs: 3
- Honey: 1/4 cup
- Vanilla Extract: 1 tsp
- Baking Soda: 1 tsp
- Cinnamon: 1 tsp
- Salt: 1/4 tsp

Method of Cooking: Baking
Procedure:

1. Preheat oven to 350°F (175°C).
2. Mix almond flour, baking soda, cinnamon, and salt.
3. In another bowl, combine bananas, eggs, honey, and vanilla.
4. Mix dry and wet ingredients.
5. Pour into loaf pan, bake for 45 minutes.

Nutritional Values:
Calories: 220 per slice
Servings: Makes 10 slices

Recipe 4: Greek Yogurt and Berry Parfait

Preparation Time:
10 minutes
Ingredients:
- Greek Yogurt: 2 cups
- Mixed Berries: 1 cup
- Granola: 1/2 cup
- Honey: 2 tbsp

Method of Cooking:
Layering

Procedure:
1. Layer Greek yogurt, berries, and granola in glasses.
2. Drizzle with honey.

Nutritional Values:
Calories: 300 per serving
Servings:
Makes 2 servings

Recipe 5: Smoked Salmon and Cream Cheese Bagels

Preparation Time:
10 minutes
Ingredients:
- Whole Grain Bagels: 4
- Cream Cheese: 1/2 cup
- Smoked Salmon: 8 oz
- Capers: 2 tbsp
- Red Onion: 1/4 cup, thinly sliced
- Fresh Dill: For garnish

Method of Cooking:

Assembling
Procedure:
1. Toast bagels, spread cream cheese.
2. Top with smoked salmon, capers, and onion.

3. Garnish with dill.
Nutritional Values:
Calories: 400 per bagel
Servings:
Makes 4 bagels

Recipe 6: Shakshuka with Feta

Preparation Time:
40 minutes
Ingredients:
• Eggs: 6
• Crushed Tomatoes: 1 can (28 oz)
• Feta Cheese: 1/2 cup, crumbled
• Onion: 1, diced
• Red Bell Pepper: 1, diced
• Garlic: 2 cloves, minced
• Paprika: 1 tsp
• Cumin: 1 tsp
• Olive Oil: 2 tbsp
• Salt and Pepper: To taste

• Cilantro: For garnish
Method of Cooking: Simmering
Procedure:
1. Sauté onion, bell pepper, and garlic in olive oil.
2. Add tomatoes, paprika, cumin, salt, and pepper.
3. Simmer for 20 minutes.
4. Crack eggs into sauce, cover, cook until eggs are set.
5. Sprinkle with feta and cilantro.
Nutritional Values:
Calories: 250 per serving
Servings: Makes 6 servings

Recipe 7: Whole Wheat Blueberry Pancakes

Preparation Time:
20 minutes
Ingredients:
• Whole Wheat Flour: 1 1/2 cups
• Fresh Blueberries: 1 cup
• Eggs: 2
• Almond Milk: 1 1/2 cups
• Maple Syrup: 2 tbsp
• Baking Powder: 1 tsp
• Vanilla Extract: 1 tsp
• Coconut Oil (for cooking): As needed
Method of Cooking:
Pan-frying
Procedure:

1. Mix flour, baking powder, and salt.
2. In another bowl, whisk eggs, almond milk, and vanilla.
3. Combine wet and dry ingredients, fold in blueberries.
4. Cook pancakes in coconut oil until golden.
Nutritional Values:
Calories: 180 per pancake
Servings:
Makes 8 pancakes

Recipe 8: Avocado and Tomato Toast with Poached Eggs

Preparation Time:
15 minutes
Ingredients:
- Sourdough Bread: 4 slices
- Avocado: 2, mashed
- Cherry Tomatoes: 1 cup, halved
- Eggs: 4, poached
- Olive Oil: 2 tbsp
- Salt and Pepper: To taste
- Fresh Basil: For garnish

Method of Cooking:
Poaching, toasting

Procedure:
1. Toast sourdough bread, spread with mashed avocado.
2. Top with tomato halves and a poached egg.
3. Drizzle with olive oil, season with salt and pepper.
4. Garnish with basil.

Nutritional Values:
Calories: 350 per toast
Servings:
Makes 4 servings

Recipe 9: Huevos Rancheros

Preparation Time:
30 minutes
Ingredients:
- Corn Tortillas: 4
- Eggs: 4
- Black Beans: 1 can (15 oz), drained
- Salsa: 1 cup
- Avocado: 1, sliced
- Feta Cheese: 1/4 cup, crumbled
- Olive Oil: 2 tbsp
- Cilantro: For garnish

Method of Cooking:
Frying, assembling

Procedure:
1. Fry eggs in olive oil.
2. Warm tortillas, spread with black beans.
3. Top each with a fried egg, salsa, and avocado.
4. Sprinkle with feta, garnish with cilantro.

Nutritional Values:
Calories: 400 per serving
Servings:
Makes 4 servings

Recipe 10: Sweet Potato and Black Bean Breakfast Burritos

Preparation Time:
45 minutes
Ingredients:
- Sweet Potatoes: 2, diced
- Black Beans: 1 can (15 oz), drained
- Eggs: 6, scrambled
- Whole Wheat Tortillas: 6
- Cheddar Cheese: 1/2 cup, shredded
- Red Onion: 1/2 cup, diced
- Cumin: 1 tsp
- Olive Oil: 2 tbsp
- Salt and Pepper: To taste

- Salsa: For serving

Method of Cooking:
Sautéing, assembling

Procedure:
1. Sauté sweet potatoes and onion in olive oil.
2. Add cumin, salt, and pepper.
3. Stir in black beans and scrambled eggs.
4. Fill tortillas with mixture, top with cheese.
1. Roll into burritos, serve with salsa.

Nutritional Values:
Calories: 450 per burrito

Servings:
Makes 6 burritos

Recipe 11: Baked Avocado Eggs

Preparation Time:
25 minutes

Ingredients:
- Avocados: 4
- Eggs: 8
- Chives: 1 tbsp, chopped
- Paprika: 1 tsp
- Salt and Pepper: To taste

Method of Cooking:
Baking

Procedure:
1. Halve avocados, remove pits.
2. Crack an egg into each avocado half.
3. Season with salt, pepper, and paprika.
4. Bake at 425°F (220°C) for 15 minutes.
5. Garnish with chives.

Nutritional Values:
Calories: 220 per half

Servings:
Makes 8 halves

Chapter 5: Lunches for Longevity

Light and Fresh Salads

Recipe 1: Arugula and Quinoa Salad with Lemon Vinaigrette

Preparation Time:
20 minutes
Ingredients:
- Arugula: 2 cups
- Quinoa (cooked): 1 cup
- Cherry Tomatoes: 1/2 cup, halved
- Cucumber: 1, diced
- Feta Cheese: 1/4 cup, crumbled
- Olive Oil: 2 tbsp
- Lemon Juice: 1 tbsp
- Salt and Pepper: To taste
Method of Cooking:
No-cook, assembling
Procedure:
1. Combine arugula, quinoa, tomatoes, and cucumber in a bowl.
2. Whisk together olive oil, lemon juice, salt, and pepper.
3. Drizzle vinaigrette over the salad, top with feta cheese.
Nutritional Values:
Calories: 250 per serving
Servings:
Makes 2 servings

Recipe 2: Mediterranean Chickpea Salad

Preparation Time:
15 minutes
Ingredients:
- Chickpeas: 1 can (15 oz), drained and rinsed
- Red Onion: 1/4 cup, finely chopped
- Bell Pepper: 1, diced
- Cucumber: 1, diced
- Parsley: 1/4 cup, chopped
- Olive Oil: 2 tbsp
- Lemon Juice: 2 tbsp
- Feta Cheese: 1/4 cup, crumbled
- Salt and Pepper: To taste
Method of Cooking:
No-cook, mixing
Procedure:
1. In a bowl, combine chickpeas, onion, bell pepper, cucumber, and parsley.
2. Dress with olive oil and lemon juice.
3. Season with salt and pepper, top with feta cheese.
Nutritional Values:
Calories: 300 per serving
Servings:
Makes 4 servings

Recipe 3: Asian Sesame Chicken Salad

Preparation Time:
30 minutes
Ingredients:
- Chicken Breast: 2, grilled and sliced
- Mixed Greens: 4 cups
- Red Cabbage: 1 cup, shredded
- Carrots: 1/2 cup, julienned
- Cucumbers: 1/2 cup, sliced
- Sesame Seeds: 1 tbsp
- Soy Sauce: 2 tbsp
- Sesame Oil: 1 tbsp
- Honey: 1 tbsp
- Rice Vinegar: 1 tbsp

Method of Cooking:
Grilling, mixing
Procedure:
1. Mix soy sauce, sesame oil, honey, and vinegar for dressing.
2. Toss greens, cabbage, carrots, and cucumbers.
3. Top with grilled chicken and sesame seeds, dress with the mixture.

Nutritional Values:
Calories: 350 per serving
Servings:
Makes 4 servings

Recipe 4: Avocado and Black Bean Salad

Preparation Time:
15 minutes
Ingredients:
- Black Beans: 1 can (15 oz), drained and rinsed
- Avocado: 1, diced
- Cherry Tomatoes: 1/2 cup, halved
- Red Onion: 1/4 cup, finely chopped
- Cilantro: 1/4 cup, chopped
- Lime Juice: 2 tbsp
- Olive Oil: 1 tbsp
- Salt and Pepper: To taste

Method of Cooking:
No-cook, tossing
Procedure:
1. Combine beans, avocado, tomatoes, onion, and cilantro.
2. Dress with lime juice and olive oil.
3. Season with salt and pepper.

Nutritional Values:
Calories: 300 per serving
Servings:
Makes 4 servings

Recipe 5: Beetroot and Goat Cheese Salad

Preparation Time:
25 minutes
Ingredients:
- Beetroot: 3, roasted and sliced
- Mixed Greens: 4 cups
- Goat Cheese: 1/3 cup, crumbled
- Walnuts: 1/4 cup, chopped
- Balsamic Vinegar: 2 tbsp
- Olive Oil: 2 tbsp
- Honey: 1 tsp
- Salt and Pepper: To taste

Method of Cooking:
Roasting, assembling
Procedure:
1. Whisk together vinegar, olive oil, honey, salt, and pepper for dressing.
2. Toss mixed greens with dressing.
3. Top with sliced beetroot, goat cheese, and walnuts.

Nutritional Values:
Calories: 350 per serving
Servings:
Makes 4 servings

Recipe 6: Grilled Vegetable and Halloumi Salad

Preparation Time:
30 minutes
Ingredients:
- Zucchini: 1, sliced
- Bell Peppers: 2, sliced
- Red Onion: 1, sliced
- Halloumi Cheese: 8 oz, sliced
- Mixed Greens: 4 cups
- Olive Oil: 2 tbsp
- Lemon Juice: 2 tbsp
- Salt and Pepper: To taste

Method of Cooking:
Grilling
Procedure:
1. Grill zucchini, peppers, onion, and halloumi until charred.
2. Toss greens with olive oil and lemon juice.
3. Arrange grilled vegetables and halloumi on top.

Nutritional Values:
Calories: 400 per serving
Servings:
Makes 4 servings

Recipe 7: Tuna Niçoise Salad

Preparation Time:
30 minutes
Ingredients:
- Tuna Steaks: 2, grilled
- Green Beans: 1 cup, blanched
- Baby Potatoes: 1 cup, boiled
- Hard-Boiled Eggs: 4, quartered
- Olives: 1/4 cup
- Mixed Greens: 4 cups
- Olive Oil: 3 tbsp
- Dijon Mustard: 1 tbsp
- Lemon Juice: 2 tbsp
- Salt and Pepper: To taste

Method of Cooking:
Grilling, boiling
Procedure:
1. Whisk together olive oil, mustard, lemon juice, salt, and pepper.
2. Toss greens with dressing.
3. Arrange tuna, green beans, potatoes, eggs, and olives on top.

Nutritional Values:
Calories: 450 per serving
Servings:

Recipe 8: Watermelon and Feta Salad

Preparation Time:
15 minutes
Ingredients:
- Watermelon: 4 cups, cubed
- Feta Cheese: 1/2 cup, crumbled
- Mint Leaves: 1/4 cup, chopped
- Red Onion: 1/4 cup, thinly sliced
- Olive Oil: 2 tbsp
- Lime Juice: 2 tbsp
- Salt and Pepper: To taste

Method of Cooking:
No-cook, assembling
Procedure:
1. Combine watermelon, feta, mint, and onion.
2. Dress with olive oil and lime juice.
3. Season lightly with salt and pepper.

Nutritional Values:
Calories: 200 per serving
Servings:
Makes 4 servings

Recipe 9: Cucumber and Dill Salad

Preparation Time:
15 minutes
Ingredients:
- Cucumber: 2, thinly sliced
- Dill: 1/4 cup, chopped
- Greek Yogurt: 1/2 cup
- Lemon Juice: 2 tbsp
- Garlic: 1 clove, minced
- Salt and Pepper: To taste

Method of Cooking:
Mixing
Procedure:
1. In a bowl, combine sliced cucumber and dill.
2. In a small bowl, mix Greek yogurt, lemon juice, garlic, salt, and pepper.
3. Pour dressing over cucumber, toss to combine.

Nutritional Values:
Calories: 100 per serving
Servings:
Makes 4 servings

Hearty Soups and Stews

Recipe 1: Mediterranean Chickpea Salad

Preparation Time:
20 minutes
Ingredients:
- Chickpeas: 1 can (15 oz), drained and rinsed
- Cucumber: 1, diced
- Cherry Tomatoes: 1 cup, halved
- Red Onion: 1/4 cup, finely chopped
- Feta Cheese: 1/2 cup, crumbled
- Kalamata Olives: 1/4 cup, pitted and sliced
- Olive Oil: 3 tbsp
- Lemon Juice: 2 tbsp
- Garlic: 1 clove, minced
- Oregano: 1 tsp, dried
- Salt and Pepper: To taste

Method of Cooking:
No-cook, mixing
Procedure:
1. Combine chickpeas, cucumber, tomatoes, onion, feta, and olives in a bowl.
2. Whisk together olive oil, lemon juice, garlic, oregano, salt, and pepper.
3. Drizzle dressing over salad, toss to combine.

Nutritional Values:
Calories: 250 per serving
Servings:
Makes 4 servings

Recipe 2: Asian-Inspired Quinoa Salad

Preparation Time:
30 minutes
Ingredients:
- Quinoa: 1 cup, cooked
- Red Cabbage: 1 cup, shredded
- Carrots: 1/2 cup, julienned
- Edamame: 1/2 cup, shelled and cooked
- Red Pepper: 1, thinly sliced
- Cilantro: 1/4 cup, chopped
- Sesame Seeds: 2 tbsp
- Soy Sauce: 2 tbsp
- Rice Vinegar: 1 tbsp
- Sesame Oil: 1 tbsp
- Honey: 1 tsp
- Ginger: 1 tsp, grated

Method of Cooking:
No-cook, mixing
Procedure:
1. In a bowl, mix quinoa, cabbage, carrots, edamame, red pepper, and cilantro.
2. Whisk together soy sauce, rice vinegar, sesame oil, honey, and ginger.
3. Pour dressing over salad, sprinkle with sesame seeds.

Nutritional Values:
Calories: 300 per serving
Servings:
Makes 4 servings

Recipe 3: Avocado and Tomato Salad

Preparation Time:
15 minutes

Ingredients:
- Avocados: 2, diced
- Cherry Tomatoes: 1 cup, halved
- Red Onion: 1/4 cup, thinly sliced
- Lime Juice: 2 tbsp
- Olive Oil: 2 tbsp
- Cilantro: 1/4 cup, chopped
- Salt and Pepper: To taste

Method of Cooking:
No-cook, mixing

Procedure:
1. Gently combine avocados, tomatoes, and onion in a bowl.
2. Whisk together lime juice, olive oil, salt, and pepper.
3. Drizzle dressing over salad, sprinkle with cilantro.

Nutritional Values:
Calories: 220 per serving

Servings:
Makes 4 servings

Recipe 4: Spinach and Strawberry Salad

Preparation Time:
20 minutes
Ingredients:
- Baby Spinach: 4 cups
- Strawberries: 1 cup, sliced
- Almonds: 1/4 cup, sliced
- Goat Cheese: 1/4 cup, crumbled
- Balsamic Vinegar: 3 tbsp
- Olive Oil: 2 tbsp
- Honey: 1 tsp
- Salt and Pepper: To taste

Method of Cooking:
No-cook, mixing

Procedure:
1. Toss spinach, strawberries, almonds, and goat cheese in a large bowl.
2. Whisk together balsamic vinegar, olive oil, honey, salt, and pepper.
3. Pour dressing over salad, toss gently.

Nutritional Values:
Calories: 200 per serving
Servings:
Makes 4 servings

Recipe 5: Beetroot and Goat Cheese Salad

Preparation Time:
45 minutes (includes roasting beets)
Ingredients:
- Beetroots: 3, roasted and sliced
- Goat Cheese: 1/2 cup, crumbled
- Arugula: 2 cups
- Walnuts: 1/4 cup, chopped
- Olive Oil: 3 tbsp
- Balsamic Vinegar: 2 tbsp
- Honey: 1 tsp
- Salt and Pepper: To taste

Method of Cooking:
Roasting, mixing

Procedure:
1. Roast beetroots, then slice.
2. Combine arugula, beetroot slices, goat cheese, and walnuts in a bowl.
3. Whisk together olive oil, balsamic vinegar, honey, salt, and pepper.
4. Drizzle dressing over salad.

Nutritional Values:
Calories: 250 per serving
Servings:
Makes 4 servings

Recipe 6: Greek Salad with Grilled Chicken

Preparation Time:
30 minutes
Ingredients:

- Chicken Breast: 2, grilled and sliced
- Cucumber: 1, diced
- Cherry Tomatoes: 1 cup, halved
- Red Onion: 1/4 cup, thinly sliced

- Kalamata Olives: 1/4 cup, pitted and sliced
- Feta Cheese: 1/2 cup, crumbled
- Olive Oil: 3 tbsp
- Lemon Juice: 2 tbsp
- Oregano: 1 tsp, dried
- Salt and Pepper: To taste

Method of Cooking:
Grilling, mixing
Procedure:
1.   Grill chicken breasts, then slice.
2.   In a bowl, mix cucumber, tomatoes, onion, olives, and feta.
3.   Whisk together olive oil, lemon juice, oregano, salt, and pepper.
4.   Toss chicken with salad, pour dressing over top.

Nutritional Values:
Calories: 350 per serving
Servings:
Makes 4 servings

Recipe 7: Watermelon and Feta Salad

Preparation Time:
20 minutes
Ingredients:
- Watermelon: 4 cups, cubed
- Feta Cheese: 1 cup, crumbled
- Mint Leaves: 1/4 cup, chopped
- Lime Juice: 3 tbsp
- Olive Oil: 2 tbsp
- Black Pepper: A pinch

Method of Cooking:
No-cook, mixing

Procedure:
1. In a large bowl, combine watermelon, feta, and mint.
2. Whisk together lime juice, olive oil, and black pepper.
3. Drizzle dressing over salad, toss gently.

Nutritional Values:
Calories: 180 per serving
Servings:
Makes 4 servings

Recipe 8: Roasted Vegetable Quinoa Salad

Preparation Time:
40 minutes
Ingredients:
- Quinoa: 1 cup, cooked
- Zucchini: 1, diced
- Red Pepper: 1, diced
- Eggplant: 1/2, diced
- Red Onion: 1/2, diced
- Olive Oil: 3 tbsp
- Balsamic Vinegar: 2 tbsp
- Garlic: 1 clove, minced
- Salt and Pepper: To taste

Method of Cooking:
Roasting, mixing
Procedure:
1. Toss vegetables with olive oil, garlic, salt, and pepper.
2. Roast at 400°F (200°C) for 30 minutes.
3. Mix roasted vegetables with cooked quinoa.
4. Drizzle with balsamic vinegar.

Nutritional Values:
Calories: 300 per serving
Servings: Makes 4 servings

Recipe 9: Pear and Walnut Salad

Preparation Time:
20 minutes
Ingredients:
- Mixed Greens: 4 cups
- Pear: 1, thinly sliced
- Walnuts: 1/4 cup, chopped
- Blue Cheese: 1/4 cup, crumbled
- Olive Oil: 3 tbsp
- Apple Cider Vinegar: 2 tbsp
- Honey: 1 tsp
- Mustard: 1 tsp
- Salt and Pepper: To taste

Method of Cooking:
No-cook, mixing

Procedure:
1. In a bowl, combine mixed greens, pear slices, walnuts, and blue cheese.
2. Whisk together olive oil, apple cider vinegar, honey, mustard, salt, and pepper.
1. Pour dressing over salad, toss to combine.

Nutritional Values:
Calories: 250 per serving
Servings:
Makes 4 servings

Recipe 10: Grilled Shrimp Caesar Salad

Preparation Time:
30 minutes
Ingredients:
- Shrimp: 1 lb., grilled
- Romaine Lettuce: 1 head, chopped
- Parmesan Cheese: 1/4 cup
- Croutons: 1 cup
- Caesar Dressing: 1/2 cup
- Lemon Juice: 1 tbsp

Procedure:
1. Grill seasoned shrimp.
2. Toss lettuce, Parmesan, croutons, and shrimp.
3. Drizzle with dressing and lemon juice.

Nutritional Values:
Calories: 350 per serving
Servings: 4

Recipe 11: Asian Sesame Tofu Salad

Preparation Time: 25 minutes
Ingredients:
- Firm Tofu: 1 block, cubed and pan-fried
- Mixed Greens: 4 cups
- Carrots: 1/2 cup, julienned
- Red Cabbage: 1/2 cup, shredded
- Cucumber: 1/2, sliced
- Sesame Seeds: 2 tbsp
- Soy Sauce, Sesame Oil, Rice Vinegar, Honey, Ginger: For dressing

Procedure:
1. Pan-fry tofu until golden.
2. Combine greens, carrots, cabbage, cucumber.
3. Toss with soy-sesame dressing.
4. Top with tofu and sesame seeds.

Nutritional Values:
Calories: 300 per serving
Servings: 4

Wraps and Sandwiches for On-the-Go

Recipe 1: Grilled Veggie Wrap

Preparation Time: 15 minutes
Ingredients:
- Whole Wheat Tortilla: 1
- Assorted Grilled Veggies (bell peppers, zucchini): 1 cup
- Hummus: 2 tbsp
- Feta Cheese: 1 tbsp

Procedure:
1. Spread hummus on tortilla.
2. Add grilled veggies, sprinkle feta.
3. Roll tightly.

Nutritional Values: ~300 calories
Servings: 1

Recipe 2: Chicken Pesto Sandwich

Preparation Time: 10 minutes
Ingredients:
- Whole Grain Bread: 2 slices
- Grilled Chicken Breast: 1, sliced
- Pesto Sauce: 1 tbsp
- Tomato: 2 slices
- Lettuce: 1 leaf

Procedure:
1. Spread pesto on bread.
2. Layer chicken, tomato, lettuce.
3. Close sandwich.

Nutritional Values: ~350 calories
Servings: 1

Recipe 3: Tuna and Avocado Wrap

Preparation Time: 10 minutes
Ingredients:
- Whole Wheat Wrap: 1
- Canned Tuna (in water): 1 can, drained
- Avocado: 1/2, mashed
- Lemon Juice: 1 tsp
- Spinach Leaves: A handful

Procedure:
1. Mix tuna, avocado, lemon.
2. Spread on wrap, add spinach.
3. Roll up tightly.

Nutritional Values: ~400 calories
Servings: 1

Recipe 4: Turkey and Cranberry Sandwich

Preparation Time: 5 minutes
Ingredients:
- Whole Grain Bread: 2 slices
- Turkey Breast: 3 slices
- Cranberry Sauce: 1 tbsp
- Lettuce: 1 leaf
- Mustard: 1 tsp

Procedure:
1. Spread cranberry and mustard on bread.
2. Add turkey, lettuce.
3. Assemble sandwich.

Nutritional Values: ~330 calories
Servings: 1

Recipe 5: Roasted Eggplant and Pepper Pita

Preparation Time: 20 minutes
Ingredients:
- Pita Bread: 1
- Eggplant: 1/2, roasted and sliced
- Red Bell Pepper: 1, roasted and sliced
- Tzatziki Sauce: 2 tbsp
- Arugula: A handful

Procedure:
1. Open pita, spread tzatziki.
2. Fill with eggplant, pepper, arugula.

Nutritional Values: ~350 calories
Servings: 1

Recipe 6: Spicy Bean Burrito

Preparation Time: 15 minutes
Ingredients:
- Whole Wheat Tortilla: 1
- Black Beans: 1/2 cup, cooked
- Salsa: 2 tbsp
- Cheddar Cheese: 1/4 cup, shredded
- Lettuce: A handful, shredded

Procedure:
1. Heat beans, mix with salsa.
2. Fill tortilla with bean mixture, cheese, lettuce.
3. Roll burrito-style.

Nutritional Values: ~400 calories
Servings: 1

Recipe 7: Mediterranean Falafel Wrap

Preparation Time: 10 minutes
Ingredients:
- Whole Wheat Pita: 1
- Falafel Balls: 3
- Greek Yogurt: 2 tbsp
- Cucumber: 1/4, sliced
- Tomato: 1/4, sliced

Procedure:
1. Stuff pita with falafel.
2. Add yogurt, cucumber, tomato.

Nutritional Values: ~350 calories
Servings: 1

Recipe 8: Caprese Sandwich

Preparation Time: 5 minutes
Ingredients:
- Ciabatta Bread: 1 small loaf
- Mozzarella Cheese:
- 2 slices
- Tomato: 2 slices
- Fresh Basil: A few leaves
- Balsamic Glaze: 1 tsp

Procedure:
1. Layer mozzarella, tomato, basil on bread.
2. Drizzle with balsamic glaze.
3. Close sandwich.

Nutritional Values: ~350 calories
Servings: 1

Recipe 9: Smoked Salmon and Cucumber Bagel

Preparation Time: 5 minutes
Ingredients:
- Whole Grain Bagel: 1
- Smoked Salmon: 2 oz
- Cream Cheese: 2 tbsp
- Cucumber: 1/4, sliced
- Dill: A pinch

Procedure:

1. Spread cream cheese on bagel.
2. Add salmon, cucumber.
3. Garnish with dill.

Nutritional Values: ~400 calories
Servings: 1

Recipe 10: BBQ Chicken Wrap

Preparation Time: 15 minutes
Ingredients:
- Whole Wheat Tortilla: 1
- Cooked Chicken Breast: 1/2, shredded
- BBQ Sauce: 2 tbsp
- Coleslaw Mix: 1/2 cup
- Cilantro: A handful

Procedure:

1. Toss chicken in BBQ sauce.
2. Fill tortilla with chicken, coleslaw.
3. Add cilantro, roll up.

Nutritional Values: ~400 calories
Servings: 1

Recipe 11: Vegan Hummus and Veggie Sandwich

Preparation Time: 10 minutes
Ingredients:
- Multi-Grain Bread: 2 slices
- Hummus: 2 tbsp
- Sliced Veggies (cucumber, bell pepper, carrot): 1/2 cup
- Spinach: A handful

Procedure:

1. **Spread hummus on bread.**
2. **Layer veggies, spinach.**
3. Assemble sandwich.

Nutritional Values: ~300 calories
Servings: 1

Chapter 6: Dinner Delights

Family-Friendly Meals

Recipe 1: Oven-Baked Lemon Herb Chicken

Preparation Time: 40 minutes
Ingredients:
- Chicken Breasts: 4
- Lemon Juice: 3 tbsp
- Olive Oil: 2 tbsp
- Garlic: 2 cloves, minced
- Mixed Herbs: 1 tsp (thyme, oregano, rosemary)

Procedure:
1. Marinate chicken in lemon, oil, garlic, herbs.
2. Bake at 375°F for 30 minutes.

Nutritional Values: ~400 calories
Servings: 4

Recipe 2: Veggie-Packed Pasta Primavera

Preparation Time: 30 minutes
Ingredients:
- Whole Wheat Pasta: 8 oz
- Assorted Veggies (bell pepper, zucchini, cherry tomatoes): 2 cups, chopped
- Olive Oil: 2 tbsp
- Parmesan Cheese: 1/4 cup, grated

Procedure:
1. Cook pasta; sauté veggies in oil.
2. Toss pasta with veggies, top with cheese.

Nutritional Values: ~350 calories
Servings: 4

Recipe 3: Quinoa Stuffed Bell Peppers

Preparation Time: 50 minutes
Ingredients:
- Bell Peppers: 4, halved
- Cooked Quinoa: 2 cups
- Black Beans: 1 can, drained
- Corn: 1 cup
- Shredded Cheese: 1/2 cup

Procedure:
1. Mix quinoa, beans, corn.
2. Stuff peppers, top with cheese.
3. Bake at 350°F for 20 minutes.

Nutritional Values: ~300 calories
Servings: 4

Recipe 4: Hearty Turkey Chili

Preparation Time: 1 hour
Ingredients:
- Ground Turkey: 1 lb
- Canned Tomatoes: 1 can (14 oz)
- Kidney Beans: 1 can, drained
- Onion: 1, chopped
- Chili Powder: 2 tbsp

Procedure:
1. Brown turkey, add onions.
2. Stir in tomatoes, beans, chili powder.
3. Simmer for 45 minutes.

Nutritional Values: ~400 calories
Servings: 4

Recipe 5: Baked Salmon with Asparagus

Preparation Time: 25 minutes
Ingredients:
- Salmon Fillets: 4
- Asparagus: 1 bunch, trimmed
- Lemon Slices: 8
- Olive Oil: 2 tbsp
- Dill: 1 tsp, dried

Procedure:
1. Place salmon, asparagus on baking sheet.
2. Top with lemon, oil, dill.
3. Bake at 400°F for 15 minutes.

Nutritional Values: ~350 calories
Servings: 4

Recipe 6: Easy Vegetable Stir-Fry

Preparation Time: 20 minutes
Ingredients:
- Mixed Vegetables: 4 cups (broccoli, bell pepper, carrots)
- Soy Sauce: 3 tbsp
- Sesame Oil: 1 tbsp
- Garlic: 1 clove, minced
- Brown Rice: 2 cups, cooked

Procedure:
1. Sauté vegetables in sesame oil and garlic.
2. Add soy sauce; serve over rice.

Nutritional Values: ~300 calories
Servings: 4

Recipe 7: Homemade Chicken Tacos

Preparation Time: 30 minutes
Ingredients:
- Chicken Breast: 2, cooked and shredded
- Whole Wheat Tortillas: 8
- Salsa: 1 cup
- Lettuce: 2 cups, shredded
- Shredded Cheese: 1/2 cup

Procedure:
1. Heat chicken, add salsa.
2. Fill tortillas with chicken, lettuce, cheese.

Nutritional Values: ~350 calories
Servings: 4

Recipe 8: Meatball and Vegetable

Preparation Time: 40 minutes
Ingredients:
- Pre-made Meatballs: 12
- Bell Peppers: 2, cut into chunks
- Zucchini: 1, sliced
- Cherry Tomatoes: 12
- Olive Oil: 2 tbsp

Procedure:
1. Skewer meatballs, peppers, zucchini, tomatoes.
2. Brush with olive oil.
3. Grill or bake until cooked through.

Nutritional Values: ~400 calories
Servings: 4

Recipe 9: Cauliflower Crust Pizza

Preparation Time: 30 minutes
Ingredients:
- Cauliflower Crust: 1 pre-made
- Pizza Sauce: 1/2 cup
- Mozzarella Cheese: 1 cup, shredded
- Assorted Toppings: bell peppers, onions, mushrooms

Procedure:
1. Spread sauce on crust.
2. Add cheese and toppings.
3. Bake at 425°F for 15 minutes.

Nutritional Values: ~350 calories per slice

Recipe 10: Lentil Soup with Vegetables

Preparation Time: 45 minutes
Ingredients:
- Lentils: 1 cup, dried
- Vegetable Broth: 4 cups
- Carrots: 1 cup, chopped
- Celery: 1 cup, chopped
- Onion: 1, diced

Procedure:
1. Cook lentils in broth with vegetables.
2. Simmer until lentils are tender.

Nutritional Values: ~250 calories
Servings: 4

Recipe 11: Baked Fish Tacos

Preparation Time: 30 minutes
Ingredients:
- White Fish Fillets: 4
- Whole Wheat Tortillas: 8
- Cabbage Slaw: 2 cups
- Greek Yogurt: 1 cup
- Lime: 2, juiced

Procedure:
1. Bake fish, flake apart.
2. Mix yogurt with lime juice.
3. Assemble tacos with fish, slaw, yogurt sauce.

Nutritional Values: ~350 calories
Servings: 4

Elegant Dinners for Two

Recipe 1: Herb-Crusted Salmon Fillets

Preparation Time: 25 minutes
Ingredients:
- Salmon Fillets: 2
- Dried Herbs (dill, parsley, thyme): 2 tbsp, mixed
- Lemon Zest: 1 tsp
- Olive Oil: 2 tbsp

Procedure:
1. Coat salmon with herbs, zest, oil.
2. Bake at 400°F for 20 minutes.

Nutritional Values: ~400 calories per serving
Servings: 2

Recipe 2: Garlic Shrimp Pasta

Preparation Time: 30 minutes
Ingredients:
- Whole Wheat Spaghetti: 6 oz
- Shrimp: 8 oz, peeled
- Garlic: 2 cloves, minced
- Olive Oil: 2 tbsp
- Parsley: 1 tbsp, chopped

Procedure:

1. Cook pasta; sauté shrimp with garlic in oil.
2. Toss pasta with shrimp, garnish with parsley.

Nutritional Values: ~450 calories per serving
Servings: 2

Recipe 3: Stuffed Bell Peppers

Preparation Time: 45 minutes
Ingredients:
- Bell Peppers: 2
- Quinoa: 1/2 cup, cooked
- Black Beans: 1/2 cup, drained
- Corn: 1/2 cup
- Shredded Cheese: 1/4 cup

Procedure:

1. Mix quinoa, beans, corn; stuff peppers.
2. Top with cheese, bake at 350°F for 25 minutes.

Nutritional Values: ~350 calories per serving
Servings: 2

Recipe 4: Lemon Butter Chicken

Preparation Time: 35 minutes
Ingredients:
- Chicken Breasts: 2
- Lemon Juice: 2 tbsp
- Butter: 2 tbsp
- Garlic: 1 clove, minced
- Thyme: 1 tsp

Procedure:

1. Sauté chicken with garlic, butter, thyme.
2. Finish with lemon juice.

Nutritional Values: ~400 calories per serving
Servings: 2

Recipe 5: Seared Scallops with Asparagus

Preparation Time: 20 minutes
Ingredients:
- Scallops: 6 large
- Asparagus: 1 bunch, trimmed
- Garlic: 1 clove, minced
- Olive Oil: 1 tbsp
- Lemon: 1, juiced

Procedure:

1. Sear scallops; sauté asparagus with garlic.
2. Serve scallops on asparagus, drizzle with lemon.

Nutritional Values: ~300 calories per serving
Servings: 2

Recipe 6: Beef Tenderloin with Roasted Vegetables

Preparation Time: 1 hour
Ingredients:
- Beef Tenderloin Steaks: 2
- Carrots: 1 cup, chopped
- Brussels Sprouts: 1 cup, halved
- Olive Oil: 2 tbsp
- Rosemary: 1 tsp, chopped

Procedure:
1. Roast vegetables with oil, rosemary.
2. Sear steaks; serve with vegetables.

Nutritional Values: ~500 calories per serving
Servings: 2

Recipe 7: Mushroom Risotto

Preparation Time: 45 minutes
Ingredients:
- Arborio Rice: 1 cup
- Mushrooms: 1 cup, sliced
- Onion: 1/2, diced
- Vegetable Broth: 3 cups
- Parmesan Cheese: 1/4 cup, grated

Procedure:
1. Sauté mushrooms, onion; add rice.
2. Gradually add broth, stirring; finish with Parmesan.

Nutritional Values: ~400 calories per serving
Servings:

Recipe 8: Grilled Vegetable Platter

Preparation Time: 30 minutes
Ingredients:
- Eggplant: 1/2, sliced
- Red Pepper: 1, sliced
- Olive Oil: 2 tbsp
- Balsamic Vinegar: 1 tbsp
- Fresh Herbs: 1 tbsp, chopped

Procedure:
1. Brush vegetables with oil and vinegar.
2. Grill until tender, sprinkle with herbs.

Nutritional Values: ~250 calories per serving
Servings: 2

Recipe 9: Balsamic Glazed Salmon

Preparation Time: 30 minutes
Ingredients:
- Salmon Fillets: 2
- Balsamic Vinegar: 3 tbsp
- Honey: 1 tbsp
- Garlic: 1 clove, minced
- Olive Oil: 1 tbsp

Procedure:
1. Mix vinegar, honey, garlic.
2. Marinate salmon, then grill.
3. Serve with glaze drizzle.

Nutritional Values: ~350 calories per serving

Servings: 2

Recipe 10: Spinach and Goat Cheese Stuffed Chicken

Preparation Time: 40 minutes

Ingredients:
- Chicken Breasts: 2, butterflied
- Spinach: 1 cup, sautéed
- Goat Cheese: 2 oz
- Garlic: 1 clove, minced
- Olive Oil: 1 tbsp

Procedure:

1. Stuff chicken with spinach, cheese.
2. Sauté with garlic and oil.
3. Bake at 375°F for 25 minutes.

Nutritional Values: ~400 calories per serving

Servings: 2

Recipe 11: Shrimp and Avocado Salad

Preparation Time: 20 minutes

Ingredients:
- Shrimp: 8 oz, cooked
- Avocado: 1, diced
- Mixed Greens: 2 cups
- Olive Oil: 2 tbsp
- Lemon Juice: 1 tbsp

Procedure:

1. Toss shrimp, avocado, greens.
2. Dress with oil and lemon.

Nutritional Values: ~300 calories per serving

Servings: 2

Vegetarian Nights

Recipe 1: Stuffed Portobello Mushrooms

Preparation Time: 30 minutes

Ingredients:
- Portobello Mushrooms: 2, large
- Spinach: 1 cup, chopped
- Feta Cheese: 1/4 cup, crumbled
- Garlic: 1 clove, minced
- Olive Oil: 1 tbsp

Procedure:

1. Sauté spinach and garlic.
2. Stuff mushrooms with spinach, top with feta.
3. Bake at 375°F for 20 minutes.

Nutritional Values: ~250 calories per serving

Servings: 2

Recipe 2: Quinoa and Black Bean Salad

Preparation Time: 20 minutes
Ingredients:
- Quinoa: 1 cup, cooked
- Black Beans: 1 can, drained
- Corn: 1/2 cup
- Red Bell Pepper: 1, diced
- Cilantro: 2 tbsp, chopped

Procedure:
1. Combine all ingredients.
2. Serve chilled or at room temperature.
Nutritional Values: ~350 calories per serving
Servings: 2

Recipe 3: Creamy Mushroom Risotto

Preparation Time: 45 minutes
Ingredients:
- Arborio Rice: 1 cup
- Mushrooms: 2 cups, sliced
- Vegetable Broth: 4 cups
- White Wine: 1/2 cup
- Parmesan Cheese: 1/4 cup, grated

Procedure:
1. Sauté mushrooms; set aside.
2. Cook rice with broth, wine; stir in mushrooms, cheese.
Nutritional Values: ~400 calories per serving
Servings: 2

Recipe 4: Eggplant Parmesan

Preparation Time: 1 hour
Ingredients:
- Eggplant: 1, sliced
- Marinara Sauce: 2 cups
- Mozzarella Cheese: 1 cup, shredded
- Parmesan Cheese: 1/2 cup, grated

- Bread Crumbs: 1/2 cup
Procedure:
1. Layer eggplant with sauce, cheeses, breadcrumbs.
2. Bake at 375°F for 45 minutes.
Nutritional Values: ~500 calories per serving
Servings:

Recipe 5: Vegetable Stir-Fry with Tofu

Preparation Time: 30 minutes
Ingredients:
- Firm Tofu: 1 block, cubed
- Mixed Vegetables: 3 cups (broccoli, bell peppers, carrots)
- Soy Sauce: 3 tbsp
- Sesame Oil: 2 tbsp
- Ginger: 1 tsp, grated

Procedure:
1. Sauté tofu until golden.
2. Add vegetables, sauce, cook until tender.
Nutritional Values: ~350 calories per serving
Servings: 2

Chapter 7: Snacks and Sides

Healthy Snack Options

Recipe 1: Greek Yogurt with Mixed Berries

Preparation Time: 5 minutes
Ingredients:
- Greek Yogurt: 1 cup
- Mixed Berries: 1/2 cup (strawberries, blueberries, raspberries)
- Honey: 1 tsp

Procedure:
1. Combine yogurt with berries.
2. Drizzle with honey.

Nutritional Values: ~200 calories per serving
Servings: 1

Recipe 2: Veggie Sticks with Hummus

Preparation Time: 10 minutes
Ingredients:
- Carrots: 1, cut into sticks
- Cucumber: 1/2, cut into sticks
- Bell Pepper: 1, sliced
- Hummus: 1/2 cup

Procedure:
1. Prepare veggie sticks.
2. Serve with hummus.

Nutritional Values: ~150 calories per serving
Servings: 2

Recipe 3: Almond Butter and Banana Toast

Preparation Time: 5 minutes
Ingredients:
- Whole Grain Bread: 2 slices
- Almond Butter: 2 tbsp
- Banana: 1, sliced

Procedure:

1. Spread almond butter on toast.
2. Top with banana slices.

Nutritional Values: ~300 calories per serving
Servings: 1

Recipe 4: Avocado and Tomato Salad

Preparation Time: 10 minutes
Ingredients:
- Avocado: 1, diced
- Tomato: 1, diced
- Lemon Juice: 1 tbsp
- Salt and Pepper: To taste

Procedure:
1. Mix avocado and tomato.
2. Season with lemon, salt, pepper.

Nutritional Values: ~250 calories per serving
Servings: 2

Recipe 5: Spiced Roasted Chickpeas

Preparation Time: 35 minutes
Ingredients:
- Chickpeas: 1 can, drained
- Olive Oil: 1 tbsp
- Paprika: 1 tsp
- Garlic Powder: 1 tsp

Procedure:
1. Toss chickpeas with oil, spices.
2. Roast at 400°F for 30 minutes.

Nutritional Values: ~180 calories per serving
Servings: 2

Recipe 6: Fruit and Nut Mix

Preparation Time: 5 minutes
Ingredients:
- Almonds: 1/4 cup
- Walnuts: 1/4 cup
- Dried Cranberries: 1/4 cup
- Pumpkin Seeds: 1/4 cup

Procedure:
- Mix all ingredients.

Nutritional Values: ~300 calories per serving
Servings: 2

Recipe 7: Cottage Cheese with Pineapple

Preparation Time: 5 minutes
Ingredients:
- Cottage Cheese: 1 cup
- Pineapple: 1/2 cup, chopped

Procedure:

Combine cottage cheese and pineapple.

Nutritional Values: ~200 calories per serving
Servings: 1

Recipe 8: Caprese Skewers

Preparation Time: 10 minutes
Ingredients:
- Cherry Tomatoes: 10
- Mozzarella Balls: 10
- Basil Leaves: 10
- Balsamic Glaze: 1 tbsp

Procedure:

1. Skewer tomato, mozzarella, basil.
2. Drizzle with balsamic glaze.

Nutritional Values: ~150 calories per serving
Servings: 2

Recipe 9: Whole Grain Crackers with Cheese

Preparation Time: 5 minutes
Ingredients:
- Whole Grain Crackers: 10
- Cheddar Cheese: 2 oz, sliced

Procedure:

1. **Pair crackers with cheese slices.**
2. **Nutritional** Values: ~250 calories per serving

Servings: 2

Recipe 10: Kale Chips

Preparation Time: 20 minutes
Ingredients:
• Kale: 1 bunch, torn into bite-size pieces
• Olive Oil: 1 tbsp
• Salt: 1/4 tsp

Procedure:
1. Toss kale with oil and salt.
2. Bake at 300°F for 15 minutes.
Nutritional Values: ~50 calories per serving
Servings: 2

Recipe 11: Greek Yogurt Parfait

Preparation Time: 10 minutes
Ingredients:
• Greek Yogurt: 1 cup
• Granola: 1/2 cup
• Honey: 1 tbsp
• Mixed Berries: 1/2 cup
Procedure:

1. Layer yogurt, granola, berries.
2. Drizzle with honey.
Nutritional Values: ~350 calories per serving
Servings: 2
Flavorful Side Dishes

Dips and Dressings

Recipe 1: Creamy Avocado Dip

Preparation Time: 10 minutes
Ingredients:
• Avocado: 1, ripe
• Greek Yogurt: 1/2 cup
• Lime Juice: 1 tbsp
• Garlic: 1 clove, minced
• Cilantro: 2 tbsp, chopped
Procedure:

1. Blend avocado, yogurt, lime, garlic.
1. Stir in cilantro.
Nutritional Values: ~200 calories per serving
Servings: 2

Recipe 2: Roasted Red Pepper Hummus

Preparation Time: 15 minutes
Ingredients:
• Chickpeas: 1 can, drained
• Roasted Red Peppers: 1/2 cup, chopped
• Tahini: 2 tbsp
• Lemon Juice: 1 tbsp

• Garlic: 1 clove, minced
Procedure:
Blend all ingredients until smooth.
Nutritional Values: ~100 calories per serving
Servings: 3

Recipe 3: Spicy Tomato Salsa

Preparation Time: 15 minutes
Ingredients:
- Tomatoes: 2, diced
- Jalapeño: 1, minced
- Onion: 1/4 cup, chopped
- Cilantro: 1/4 cup, chopped
- Lime Juice: 1 tbsp

Procedure:
Combine all ingredients.
Nutritional Values: ~50 calories per serving
Servings: 4

Chapter 8: Sweet Indulgences

Guilt-Free Desserts

Recipe 1: Baked Apple with Cinnamon

Preparation Time: 30 minutes
Ingredients:
- Apples: 2, cored
- Cinnamon: 1 tsp
- Honey: 2 tbsp
- Walnuts: 1/4 cup, chopped

Procedure:

1. Stuff apples with cinnamon, honey, walnuts.
2. Bake at 350°F for 25 minutes.

Nutritional Values: ~200 calories per serving
Servings: 2

Recipe 2: Berry Yogurt Parfait

Preparation Time: 10 minutes
Ingredients:
- Greek Yogurt: 1 cup
- Mixed Berries: 1 cup (strawberries, blueberries, raspberries)
- Granola: 1/4 cup
- Honey: 1 tbsp

Procedure:

1. Layer yogurt, berries, granola in glasses.
2. Drizzle with honey.

Nutritional Values: ~250 calories per serving
Servings: 2

Recipe 3: Dark Chocolate Avocado Mousse

Preparation Time: 15 minutes
Ingredients:
- Avocado: 1, ripe
- Dark Chocolate: 2 oz, melted
- Cocoa Powder: 2 tbsp
- Maple Syrup: 2 tbsp

Procedure:
Blend avocado, chocolate, cocoa, syrup until smooth.

Nutritional Values: ~300 calories per serving
Servings: 2

Recipe 4: Almond Flour Brownies

Preparation Time: 35 minutes

Ingredients:
- Almond Flour: 1 cup
- Cocoa Powder: 1/4 cup
- Eggs: 2
- Coconut Oil: 1/4 cup, melted
- Maple Syrup: 1/4 cup

Procedure:
1. Mix ingredients, pour into pan.
2. Bake at 350°F for 25 minutes.

Nutritional Values: ~180 calories per serving, Servings: 9

Recipe 5: No-Bake Peanut Butter Bars

Preparation Time: 1 hour (includes chilling)

Ingredients:
- Peanut Butter: 1/2 cup
- Oats: 1 cup, rolled
- Honey: 1/3 cup
- Dark Chocolate Chips: 1/4 cup

Procedure:
1. Mix peanut butter, oats, honey.
2. Press into pan, top with chocolate.
3. Chill until set.

Nutritional Values: ~200 calories per serving

Servings: 8

Recipe 6: Coconut Chia Pudding

Preparation Time: 4 hours (includes chilling)

Ingredients:
- Chia Seeds: 1/4 cup
- Coconut Milk: 1 cup
- Maple Syrup: 2 tbsp
- Vanilla Extract: 1 tsp

Procedure:
Mix all ingredients, refrigerate until thick.

Nutritional Values: ~250 calories per serving

Servings: 2

Recipe 7: Baked Pear with Honey and Walnuts

Preparation Time: 30 minutes

Ingredients:
- Pears: 2, halved
- Honey: 2 tbsp
- Walnuts: 1/4 cup, chopped
- Cinnamon: 1 tsp

Procedure:
1. Place pears on baking sheet, top with honey, walnuts, cinnamon.
2. Bake at 350°F for 20 minutes.

Nutritional Values: ~220 calories per serving

Servings: 2

Recipe 8: Greek Yogurt Chocolate Mousse

Preparation Time: 15 minutes
Ingredients:
- Greek Yogurt: 1 cup
- Dark Chocolate: 2 oz, melted
- Cocoa Powder: 1 tbsp
- Honey: 1 tbsp

Procedure:

1. Mix yogurt with melted chocolate, cocoa, honey.
2. Nutritional Values: ~280 calories per serving

Servings: 2

9: Fruit Salad with Mint and Lime

Preparation Time: 15 minutes
Ingredients:
- Mixed Fruit (strawberries, kiwi, mango, grapes): 3 cups, chopped
- Fresh Mint: 2 tbsp, chopped
- Lime Juice: 2 tbsp
- Honey: 1 tbsp

Procedure:
Toss fruit with mint, lime juice, and honey.
Nutritional Values: ~120 calories per serving
Servings: 2

Recipe 10: Banana Oat Cookies

Preparation Time: 25 minutes
Ingredients:
- Bananas: 2, ripe, mashed
- Rolled Oats: 1 cup
- Dark Chocolate Chips: 1/4 cup
- Cinnamon: 1 tsp

Procedure:

1. Mix bananas with oats, chocolate chips, cinnamon.
2. Spoon onto baking sheet, bake at 350°F for 15 minutes.

Nutritional Values: ~150 calories per serving
Servings: 6

Recipe 11: Lemon Raspberry Sorbet

Preparation Time: 2 hours (includes freezing)
Ingredients:
- Raspberries: 2 cups, frozen
- Lemon Juice: 2 tbsp
- Honey: 3 tbsp

Procedure:

1. Blend raspberries, lemon juice, and honey until smooth.
2. Freeze until set.

Nutritional Values: ~100 calories per serving
Servings: 2

Baked Goods and Pastries

Recipe 1: Almond Flour Blueberry Muffins

Preparation Time: 30 minutes
Ingredients:
- Almond Flour: 2 cups
- Eggs: 3
- Honey: 1/4 cup
- Vanilla Extract: 1 tsp
- Blueberries: 1 cup

Procedure:
1. Mix flour, eggs, honey, vanilla.
2. Fold in blueberries, bake at 350°F for 20 minutes.

Nutritional Values: ~200 calories per muffin
Servings: 12 muffins

Recipe 2: Carrot and Walnut Bread

Preparation Time: 1 hour
Ingredients:
- Grated Carrot: 1 cup
- Whole Wheat Flour: 1 1/2 cups
- Eggs: 2
- Olive Oil: 1/2 cup
- Chopped Walnuts: 1/2 cup

Procedure:
1. Combine all ingredients, pour into loaf pan.
2. Bake at 350°F for 45 minutes.

Nutritional Values: ~250 calories per slice
Servings: 10 slices

Recipe 3: Gluten-Free Banana Bread

Preparation Time: 1 hour
Ingredients:
1. Ripe Bananas: 3, mashed
2. Gluten-Free Flour: 2 cups
3. Eggs: 2
4. Coconut Oil: 1/2 cup, melted
5. Maple Syrup: 1/4 cup

Procedure:
1. Mix bananas, flour, eggs, oil, syrup.
2. Bake at 350°F for 50 minutes.

Nutritional Values: ~220 calories per slice
Servings: 12 slices

Recipe 4: Zucchini Chocolate Chip Cookies

Preparation Time: 25 minutes
Ingredients:
1. Grated Zucchini: 1 cup
2. Almond Flour: 1 1/2 cups
3. Eggs: 1
4. Coconut Oil: 1/4 cup
5. Dark Chocolate Chips: 1/2 cup

Procedure:
1. Combine zucchini, flour, egg, oil.
2. Stir in chocolate chips, bake at 350°F for 15 minutes.

Nutritional Values: ~150 calories per cookie
Servings: 15 cookies

Recipe 5: Pumpkin Spice Muffins

Preparation Time: 35 minutes
Ingredients:
- Pumpkin Puree: 1 cup
- Whole Wheat Flour: 2 cups
- Eggs: 2
- Maple Syrup: 1/2 cup
- Pumpkin Pie Spice: 1 tsp

Procedure:

1. Mix pumpkin, flour, eggs, syrup, spice.
2. Bake at 375°F for 20 minutes.

Nutritional Values: ~180 calories per muffin
Servings: 12 muffins

Recipe 6: Apple Cinnamon Scones

Preparation Time: 40 minutes
Ingredients:
- Whole Wheat Flour: 2 cups
- Diced Apple: 1 cup
- Eggs: 1
- Honey: 1/4 cup
- Cinnamon: 1 tsp

Procedure: Combine flour, apple, egg, honey, cinnamon.
1. Shape into scones, bake at 375°F for 25 minutes.

Nutritional Values: ~200 calories per scone
Servings
: 8 scones

Recipe 7: Oatmeal Raisin Cookies

Preparation Time: 20 minutes
Ingredients:
- Rolled Oats: 1 1/2 cups
- Raisins: 1/2 cup
- Eggs: 1
- Coconut Oil: 1/4 cup
- Maple Syrup: 1/4 cup

Procedure:
1. **Mix oats, raisins, egg, oil, syrup.**
2. **Bake** at 350°F for 12 minutes.

Nutritional Values: ~120 calories per cookie
Servings: 15 cookies

Recipe 8: Lemon Poppy Seed Loaf

Preparation Time: 1 hour
Ingredients:
- Whole Wheat Flour: 2 cups
- Eggs: 2
- Olive Oil: 1/2 cup
- Lemon Juice: 1/4 cup
- Poppy Seeds: 2 tbsp

Procedure:

1. Mix flour, eggs, oil, lemon juice, poppy seeds.
2. Pour into loaf pan, bake at 350°F for 45 minutes.

Nutritional Values: ~250 calories per slice
Servings: 10 slices

Recipe 9: Gluten-Free Almond Biscotti

Preparation Time: 1 hour 15 minutes
Ingredients:
- Almond Flour: 2 cups
- Eggs: 2
- Honey: 1/4 cup
- Almonds: 1/2 cup, chopped
- Vanilla Extract: 1 tsp

Procedure:

1. Combine ingredients, form into a log.
2. Bake, slice, and bake again until crisp.

Nutritional Values: ~180 calories per biscotti
Servings: 12 biscotti

Recipe 10: Pear and Ginger Muffins

Preparation Time: 35 minutes
Ingredients:
- Whole Wheat Flour: 2 cups
- Diced Pear: 1 cup
- Eggs: 2
- Coconut Oil: 1/4 cup
- Ground Ginger: 1 tsp

Procedure:

1. Mix flour, pear, eggs, oil, ginger.
2. Bake at 350°F for 20 minutes.

Nutritional Values: ~200 calories per muffin
Servings: 12 muffins

Recipe 11: Dark Chocolate Raspberry Tart

Preparation Time: 1 hour 30 minutes (includes chilling)
Ingredients:
- Almond Flour: 1 1/2 cups
- Dark Chocolate: 4 oz, melted
- Raspberries: 1 cup
- Coconut Milk: 1/2 cup
- Honey: 2 tbsp

Procedure:

1. Press almond flour into tart pan; bake.
2. Mix melted chocolate with coconut milk, honey; pour over crust.
3. Top with raspberries; chill.

Sweet Snacks

Recipe 1: Coconut and Almond Energy Balls

Preparation Time: 20 minutes
Ingredients:
• Unsweetened Shredded Coconut: 1 cup
• Almonds: 1/2 cup, ground
• Dates: 1/2 cup, pitted
• Coconut Oil: 1 tbsp

Procedure:
1. Blend almonds, dates, and oil.
2. Form into balls, roll in coconut.
Nutritional Values: ~100 calories per ball
Servings: 10 balls

Recipe 2: Baked Cinnamon Apple Chips

Preparation Time: 2 hours
Ingredients:
• Apples: 2, thinly sliced
• Cinnamon: 1 tsp
Procedure:

1. Lay apple slices on baking sheet, sprinkle with cinnamon.
2. Bake at 200°F for 2 hours.
Nutritional Values: ~50 calories per serving, Servings: 4

Recipe 3: Dark Chocolate Covered Strawberries

Preparation Time: 15 minutes
Ingredients:
• Strawberries: 1 cup
• Dark Chocolate: 2 oz, melted
Procedure:

1. Dip strawberries in chocolate.
2. Chill until set.
Nutritional Values: ~100 calories per serving
Servings: 2

Recipe 4: Greek Yogurt and Honey Popsicles

Preparation Time: 4 hours (includes freezing)
Ingredients:
• Greek Yogurt: 2 cups
• Honey: 3 tbsp
• Vanilla Extract: 1 tsp

Procedure:
1. Mix yogurt, honey, vanilla.
1. Freeze in popsicle molds.
Nutritional Values: ~150 calories per popsicle
Servings: 6 popsicles

Recipe 5: No-Bake Oatmeal Raisin Balls

Preparation Time: 15 minutes
Ingredients:
- Rolled Oats: 1 cup
- Raisins: 1/2 cup
- Peanut Butter: 1/4 cup
- Honey: 1/4 cup

Procedure:

1. Mix all ingredients, form into balls.
2. Chill to set.

Nutritional Values: ~100 calories per ball
Servings: 10 bales

Recipe 6: Roasted Spiced Nuts

Preparation Time: 20 minutes
Ingredients:
- Mixed Nuts: 2 cups
- Olive Oil: 1 tbsp
- Paprika: 1 tsp
- Garlic Powder: 1 tsp

Procedure:

1. Toss nuts with oil, spices.
2. Roast at 350°F for 15 minutes.

Nutritional Values: ~200 calories per serving
Servings: 4

Recipe 7: Banana Peanut Butter Bites

Preparation Time: 10 minutes
Ingredients:
- Banana: 1, sliced
- Peanut Butter: 1/4 cup
- Dark Chocolate Chips: 1/4 cup

Procedure:

1. Sandwich banana slices with peanut butter, top with chocolate.
2. Freeze to set.

Nutritional Values: ~100 calories per serving, **Servings:** 2

Recipe 8: Zucchini Chocolate Bread

Preparation Time: 1 hour
Ingredients:
- Grated Zucchini: 1 cup
- Whole Wheat Flour: 1 1/2 cups
- Cocoa Powder: 1/4 cup
- Eggs: 2
- Honey: 1/2 cup

Procedure:

1. Mix zucchini, flour, cocoa, eggs, honey.
2. Bake at 350°F for 45 minutes.

Nutritional Values: ~200 calories per slice
Servings: 10 slices

Recipe 9: Avocado Chocolate Mousse

Preparation Time: 15 minutes
Ingredients:
- Avocado: 1, ripe
- Cocoa Powder: 1/4 cup
- Maple Syrup: 1/4 cup
- Vanilla Extract: 1 tsp

Procedure:

1. Blend avocado, cocoa powder, maple syrup, and vanilla until smooth.
2. Chill before serving.

Nutritional Values: ~250 calories per serving
Servings: 2

Recipe 10: Pumpkin Seed and Cranberry Trail Mix

Preparation Time: 5 minutes
Ingredients:
- Pumpkin Seeds: 1/2 cup
- Dried Cranberries: 1/2 cup
- Almonds: 1/4 cup
- Dark Chocolate Chips: 1/4 cup

Procedure:

1. Mix all ingredients together.
2. Nutritional Values: ~200 calories per serving

Servings: 4

Recipe 11: Chia Seed Pudding with Mixed Berries

Preparation Time: 4 hours (includes chilling)
Ingredients:
- Chia Seeds: 1/4 cup
- Almond Milk: 1 cup
- Honey: 2 tbsp
- Mixed Berries: 1/2 cup

Procedure:

1. Mix chia seeds with almond milk and honey.
2. Refrigerate until set, top with berries.

Nutritional Values: ~150 calories per serving
Servings: 2

Chapter 9: Global Inspirations

International Cuisine Made Easy

Recipe 1: Mediterranean Quinoa Salad

Preparation Time: 20 minutes
Ingredients:
- Quinoa: 1 cup, cooked
- Cherry Tomatoes: 1/2 cup, halved
- Cucumber: 1/2, diced
- Feta Cheese: 1/4 cup, crumbled
- Kalamata Olives: 1/4 cup, sliced

Procedure:
1. Combine all ingredients.
2. Dress with olive oil and lemon juice.

Nutritional Values: ~350 calories per serving
Servings: 2

Recipe 2: Easy Chicken Tikka Masala

Preparation Time: 30 minutes
Ingredients:
- Chicken Breast: 2, cubed
- Yogurt: 1/2 cup
- Tomato Puree: 1 cup
- Garam Masala: 1 tbsp
- Garlic: 2 cloves, minced

Procedure:

1. Marinate chicken in yogurt and spices.
2. Cook with tomato puree until done.

Nutritional Values: ~400 calories per serving
Servings: 2

Recipe 3: Vegetable Pad Thai

Preparation Time: 20 minutes
Ingredients:
- Rice Noodles: 8 oz
- Assorted Vegetables (carrots, bell peppers, bean sprouts): 2 cups
- Peanut Sauce: 1/2 cup
- Peanuts: 1/4 cup, crushed
- Cilantro: 2 tbsp, chopped

Procedure:

1. Cook noodles; stir-fry vegetables.
2. **Toss with peanut sauce and top with peanuts, cilantro.**

Nutritional Values: ~450 calories per serving
Servings: 2

Recipe 4: Mexican Black Bean Stew

Preparation Time: 40 minutes
Ingredients:
- Black Beans: 1 can, drained
- Tomatoes: 1 can, diced
- Onion: 1, diced
- Cumin: 1 tsp
- Avocado: 1, diced

Procedure:

1. Cook beans with tomatoes, onion, spices.
2. Serve topped with avocado.

Nutritional Values: ~300 calories per serving
Servings: 2

Recipe 5: Italian Zucchini Noodles with Pesto

Preparation Time: 15 minutes
Ingredients:
- Zucchini: 2, spiralized
- Pesto: 1/4 cup
- Cherry Tomatoes: 1/2 cup, halved
- Parmesan Cheese: 1/4 cup, grated

Procedure:

1. Toss zucchini noodles with pesto.
2. Top with tomatoes and cheese.

Nutritional Values: ~250 calories per serving
Servings: 2

Fusion Flavors

Recipe 1: Thai-Inspired Quinoa Bowl

Preparation Time: 30 minutes
Ingredients:
- Quinoa: 1 cup, cooked
- Grilled Chicken: 1 breast, sliced
- Peanut Sauce: 1/4 cup
- Cucumber: 1/2, sliced
- Carrot: 1, julienned

Procedure:
1. Top quinoa with chicken, vegetables.
2. Drizzle with peanut sauce.

Nutritional Values: ~400 calories per serving
Servings: 2

Recipe 2: Italian-Mexican Fusion Tacos

Preparation Time: 20 minutes
Ingredients:
- Corn Tortillas: 4
- Ground Turkey: 1/2 lb, cooked
- Marinara Sauce: 1/2 cup
- Mozzarella Cheese: 1/2 cup, shredded
- Basil: Fresh, for garnish

Procedure:
1. Fill tortillas with turkey, top with marinara, cheese.
2. Bake until cheese melts, garnish with basil.

Nutritional Values: ~350 calories per serving
Servings: 2

Recipe 3: Asian-Fusion Salmon Salad

Preparation Time: 25 minutes
Ingredients:
- Salmon Fillet: 1, grilled
- Mixed Greens: 2 cups
- Soy Sauce: 2 tbsp
- Ginger: 1 tsp, grated
- Sesame Seeds: 1 tbsp

Procedure:
1. Place salmon on greens.
2. Whisk soy sauce with ginger, drizzle over salad.
3. Sprinkle with sesame seeds.

Nutritional Values: ~400 calories per serving
Servings: 2

Recipe 4: Mediterranean-Asian Shrimp Stir-Fry

Preparation Time: 20 minutes
Ingredients:
- Shrimp: 8 oz, peeled
- Olives: 1/4 cup, sliced
- Feta Cheese: 1/4 cup, crumbled
- Tomatoes: 1/2 cup, diced
- Soy Sauce: 1 tbsp

Procedure:
1. Stir-fry shrimp with tomatoes, olives.
2. Add soy sauce, top with feta.
3. Nutritional Values: ~300 calories per serving

Servings: 2

Recipe 5: Indian-Italian Spice Infused Pizza

Preparation Time: 30 minutes
Ingredients:
- Pizza Dough: 1 pre-made crust
- Tandoori Chicken: 1/2 cup, cooked and sliced
- Tomato Sauce: 1/2 cup
- Mozzarella Cheese: 1 cup, shredded
- Cilantro: 2 tbsp, chopped

Procedure:
1. Top dough with sauce, chicken, cheese.
2. Bake as directed, garnish with cilantro.

Nutritional Values: ~500 calories per serving
Servings: 2-3

Exotic Spices and Herbs

Recipe 1: Thai Basil Stir-Fry

Preparation Time: 20 minutes
Ingredients:
- Ground Beef: 1/2 lb
- Thai Basil Leaves: 1 cup
- Fish Sauce: 2 tbsp
- Soy Sauce: 1 tbsp
- Red Chili: 1, sliced

Procedure:
1. Stir-fry beef with sauces and chili.
2. Add basil at the end.

Nutritional Values: ~350 calories per serving
Servings: 2

Recipe 2: Indian Turmeric Cauliflower Rice

Preparation Time: 25 minutes
Ingredients:
- Cauliflower: 1 head, riced
- Turmeric: 1 tsp
- Cumin Seeds: 1 tsp
- Frozen Peas: 1/2 cup
- Coconut Oil: 1 tbsp

Procedure:
1. Sauté cauliflower rice with turmeric, cumin.
2. Add peas and cook until tender.

Nutritional Values: ~150 calories per serving
Servings: 2

Recipe 3: Mexican Cilantro Lime Rice

Preparation Time: 30 minutes
Ingredients:
- Basmati Rice: 1 cup
- Fresh Cilantro: 1/2 cup, chopped
- Lime Juice: 2 tbsp
- Garlic: 1 clove, minced
- Olive Oil: 1 tbsp

Procedure:
1. Cook rice with garlic, oil.
2. Stir in cilantro and lime juice.

Nutritional Values: ~200 calories per serving
Servings: 2

Recipe 4: Ethiopian Berbere Spiced Lentils

Preparation Time: 1 hour
Ingredients:
- Lentils: 1 cup, dried
- Berbere Spice Mix: 2 tbsp
- Onion: 1, diced
- Tomatoes: 1 cup, diced
- Vegetable Broth: 2 cups

Procedure:
Cook lentils with spices, onion, tomatoes in broth.

Nutritional Values: ~250 calories per serving
Servings: 4

Chapter 10: Holiday and Special Occasion Recipes

Festive Feasts

Recipe 1: Herb-Roasted Turkey Breast

Preparation Time: 2 hours
Ingredients:
- Turkey Breast: 3 lbs.
- Fresh Thyme: 1 tbsp, chopped
- Fresh Rosemary: 1 tbsp, chopped
- Garlic: 3 cloves, minced
- Olive Oil: 2 tbsp

Procedure:
1. Rub turkey with herbs, garlic, and oil.
2. Roast at 350°F until cooked through.

Nutritional Values: ~300 calories per serving
Servings: 6

Recipe 2: Quinoa and Cranberry Stuffing

Preparation Time: 40 minutes
Ingredients:
- Quinoa: 2 cups, cooked
- Dried Cranberries: 1/2 cup
- Celery: 1/2 cup, chopped
- Onion: 1/2 cup, chopped
- Chicken Broth: 1 cup

Procedure:
1. Sauté celery and onion.
2. Mix with quinoa, cranberries, broth; bake until set.

Nutritional Values: ~200 calories per serving
Servings: 4

Recipe 3: Baked Salmon with Dill Sauce

Preparation Time: 30 minutes
Ingredients:
- Salmon Fillets: 4
- Fresh Dill: 1/4 cup, chopped
- Greek Yogurt: 1/2 cup
- Lemon Juice: 2 tbsp
- Garlic: 1 clove, minced
Procedure:

1. Bake salmon at 375°F for 20 minutes.
2. Mix dill, yogurt, lemon, garlic for sauce.

Nutritional Values: ~350 calories per serving
Servings: 4

Recipe 4: Roasted Vegetable Medley

Preparation Time: 45 minutes
Ingredients:
- Assorted Vegetables (carrots, Brussels sprouts, bell peppers): 4 cups, chopped
- Olive Oil: 2 tbsp
- Garlic Powder: 1 tsp
- Thyme: 1 tsp, dried

Procedure:
1. Toss vegetables with oil, garlic, thyme.
2. Roast at 400°F until tender.

Nutritional Values: ~150 calories per serving

Servings: 4

Recipe 5: Garlic Mashed Cauliflower

Preparation Time: 30 minutes
Ingredients:
- Cauliflower: 1 head, cut into florets
- Garlic: 2 cloves, minced
- Olive Oil: 1 tbsp
- Parmesan Cheese: 1/4 cup, grated

Procedure:
1. Steam cauliflower until soft.
2. Mash with garlic, oil, Parmesan.

Nutritional Values: ~100 calories per serving

Servings: 4

Recipe 6: Spiced Sweet Potato Casserole

Preparation Time: 1 hour
Ingredients:
- Sweet Potatoes: 4, peeled and cubed
- Cinnamon: 1 tsp
- Nutmeg: 1/2 tsp
- Maple Syrup: 2 tbsp
- Pecans: 1/2 cup, chopped

Procedure:
1. Boil sweet potatoes, mash with spices, syrup.
2. Top with pecans, bake at 350°F for 20 minutes.

Nutritional Values: ~250 calories per serving

Servings: 6

Recipe 7: Grilled Asparagus with Lemon Zest

Preparation Time: 15 minutes
Ingredients:
- Asparagus: 1 lb
- Olive Oil: 2 tbsp
- Lemon Zest: 1 tbsp
- Salt and Pepper: To taste

Procedure:
1. Grill asparagus with oil.
2. Sprinkle with lemon zest, salt, pepper.

Nutritional Values: ~50 calories per serving

Servings: 4

Recipe 8: Pomegranate Glazed Brussels Sprouts

Preparation Time: 30 minutes
Ingredients:
- Brussels Sprouts: 2 cups, halved
- Pomegranate Juice: 1/2 cup
- Honey: 2 tbsp
- Balsamic Vinegar: 1 tbsp
- Olive Oil: 1 tbsp

Procedure:

1. Toss Brussels sprouts with oil, roast at 400°F for 20 minutes.
2. Glaze with a mix of pomegranate juice, honey, and vinegar.

Nutritional Values: ~150 calories per serving
Servings: 4

Recipe 9: Herb-Crusted Rack of Lamb

Preparation Time: 1 hour
Ingredients:
- Rack of Lamb: 1
- Rosemary: 2 tbsp, chopped
- Thyme: 1 tbsp, chopped
- Garlic: 3 cloves, minced
- Olive Oil: 2 tbsp

Procedure:

1. Rub lamb with herbs, garlic, oil.
2. Roast at 375°F until desired doneness.

Nutritional Values: ~400 calories per serving
Servings: 4

Recipe 10: Stuffed Portobello Mushrooms

Preparation Time: 40 minutes
Ingredients:
- Portobello Mushrooms: 4, stems removed
- Spinach: 2 cups, chopped
- Feta Cheese: 1/2 cup, crumbled
- Pine Nuts: 1/4 cup
- Garlic: 1 clove, minced

Procedure:

1. Sauté spinach and garlic, stuff mushrooms.
2. Top with feta and pine nuts, bake at 350°F for 20 minutes.

Nutritional Values: ~200 calories per serving
Servings: 4

Recipe 11: Baked Cod with Olive Tapenade

Preparation Time: 30 minutes
Ingredients:
- Cod Fillets: 4
- Olives: 1/2 cup, pitted and chopped
- Capers: 1 tbsp
- Lemon Juice: 2 tbsp
- Parsley: 2 tbsp, chopped

Procedure:

1. Top cod with a mix of olives, capers, lemon, parsley.
2. Bake at 375°F for 15 minutes.

Nutritional Values: ~250 calories per serving

Celebratory Treats

Recipe 1: Midnight Berry Delight

Preparation Time: 20 mins
Ingredients
- Blackberries, 100g
- Raspberries, 100g
- Agave syrup, 2 tbsp
- Almond flour, 150g
- Coconut oil, 50g

Method of Cooking: Baking
Procedure:
1. Blend berries and agave.
2. Mix almond flour with melted coconut oil.
3. Combine berry mix with flour mixture.
4. Bake for 15 mins at 180°C.

Nutritional Values:
Calories: 250 per serving
Carbs: 30g
Servings: 4

Recipe 2: Sunshine Citrus Salad

Preparation Time: 15 mins
Ingredients:
- Orange slices, 150g
- Lemon zest, 1 tsp
- Honey, 3 tbsp
- Mint leaves, 5g
- Quinoa, cooked, 200g

Method of Cooking: Tossing
Procedure:
1. Combine orange slices with lemon zest.
2. Add honey and mint to the mix.
3. Toss with cooked quinoa.

Nutritional Values:
Calories: 180 per serving
Protein: 8g
Servings:2

Recipe 3: Fiesta Bean Dip

Preparation Time: 30 mins
Ingredients:
- Black beans, canned, 200g
- Avocado, mashed, 100g
- Lime juice, 2 tbsp
- Cumin powder, 1 tsp
- Greek yogurt, 50g

Method of Cooking: Blending
Procedure:
1. Blend black beans until smooth.
2. Mix in mashed avocado and lime juice.
3. Stir in cumin and Greek yogurt.

Nutritional Values:

1. Calories: 200 per serving
2. Fiber: 10g

Servings: 3

Recipe 4: Gingered Carrot Soup

Preparation Time: 40 mins
Ingredients:
- Carrots, diced, 300g
- Ginger, minced, 1 tbsp
- Vegetable broth, 500ml
- Coconut milk, 100ml
- Chives, chopped, for garnish

Method of Cooking: Simmering
Procedure:
1. Sauté carrots and ginger.
2. Add broth and simmer until carrots are tender.
3. Blend until smooth, stir in coconut milk.
4. Garnish with chives.

Nutritional Values:
Calories: 150 per serving
Vitamin A: 70% DV
Servings: 4

Recipe 5: Spiced Nut Clusters

Preparation Time: 25 mins
Ingredients:
- Mixed nuts, 200g
- Cinnamon, 1 tsp
- Nutmeg, 0.5 tsp
- Maple syrup, 3 tbsp
- Sea salt, a pinch

Method of Cooking: Baking
Procedure:
1. Toss nuts with cinnamon, nutmeg, and salt.
2. Drizzle with maple syrup.
3. Bake for 10 mins at 160°C.

Nutritional Values:
Calories: 220 per serving
Healthy Fats: 15g
Servings: 5

Special Occasion Menus

Recipe 1: Grilled Salmon with Mango Salsa

Preparation Time: 30 minutes
Ingredients:
- Salmon Fillets: 4
- Mango: 1, diced
- Red Bell Pepper: 1/2, diced
- Red Onion: 1/4 cup, finely chopped
- Cilantro: 1/4 cup, chopped

Procedure:
1. Grill salmon until cooked.
2. Combine mango, pepper, onion, cilantro for salsa.

Nutritional Values: ~350 calories per serving

Servings: 4

Recipe 2: Rosemary Garlic Beef Tenderloin

Preparation Time: 1 hour
Ingredients:
- Beef Tenderloin: 2 lbs.
- Fresh Rosemary: 2 tbsp, chopped
- Garlic: 4 cloves, minced
- Olive Oil: 2 tbsp
- Salt and Pepper: To taste

Procedure:
1. Rub beef with rosemary, garlic, oil, salt, pepper.
2. Roast at 375°F until desired doneness.
3. Nutritional Values: ~400 calories per serving

Servings: 6

Recipe 3: Stuffed Bell Peppers with Quinoa and Vegetables

Preparation Time: 45 minutes
Ingredients:
- Bell Peppers: 4, halved and seeded
- Quinoa: 1 cup, cooked
- Spinach: 1 cup, chopped
- Feta Cheese: 1/2 cup, crumbled
- Cherry Tomatoes: 1/2 cup, halved

Procedure:
1. Stuff peppers with quinoa, spinach, feta, tomatoes.
2. Bake at 350°F for 20 minutes.

Nutritional Values: ~250 calories per serving
Servings: 4

Recipe 4: Lemon Herb Roasted Chicken

Preparation Time: 1 hour 30 minutes
Ingredients:
- Whole Chicken: 1 (about 4 lbs.)
- Lemon: 1, sliced
- Fresh Thyme: 1/4 cup
- Fresh Rosemary: 1/4 cup
- Garlic: 4 cloves, minced

Procedure:
1. Stuff chicken with lemon, thyme, rosemary.
2. Rub with garlic, roast at 350°F.

Nutritional Values: ~450 calories per serving
Servings: 6

Recipe 5: Vegetable and Goat Cheese Tart

Preparation Time: 1 hour
Ingredients:
- Puff Pastry: 1 sheet
- Zucchini: 1, sliced
- Tomato: 1, sliced
- Goat Cheese: 4 oz
- Basil Leaves: 1/4 cup

Procedure:
1. Layer pastry with zucchini, tomato, goat cheese.
2. Bake at 375°F for 25 minutes.

Nutritional Values: ~350 calories per serving
Servings: 4

Recipe 6: Spiced Butternut Squash Soup

Preparation Time: 45 minutes
Ingredients:
- Butternut Squash: 1, peeled and cubed
- Onion: 1, chopped
- Ginger: 1 tsp, grated
- Coconut Milk: 1 cup
- Vegetable Broth: 4 cups

Procedure:
1. Sauté onion, add squash, ginger, broth.

2. Blend until smooth, stir in coconut milk.

Nutritional Values: ~200 calories per serving

Servings: 4

Recipe 7: Quinoa and Black Bean Salad

Preparation Time: 30 minutes

Ingredients:
- Quinoa: 1 cup, cooked
- Black Beans: 1 can, drained and rinsed
- Corn: 1 cup, cooked
- Avocado: 1, diced
- Lime Juice: 2 tbsp

Procedure:
1. Mix quinoa, beans, corn, avocado.
2. Dress with lime juice, salt, pepper.

Nutritional Values: ~250 calories per serving

Servings: 4

Recipe 8: Mediterranean Vegetable Kebabs

Preparation Time: 30 minutes (plus marinating time)

Ingredients:
- Zucchini: 2, cut into chunks
- Red Bell Pepper: 1, cut into chunks
- Cherry Tomatoes: 1 cup
- Red Onion: 1, cut into chunks
- Olive Oil: 2 tbsp

- Balsamic Vinegar: 1 tbsp

Procedure:
1. Marinate vegetables in olive oil and vinegar.
2. Thread onto skewers and grill until tender.

Nutritional Values: ~150 calories per serving

Servings: 4 skewers

Recipe 9: Garlic Butter Shrimp with Herbs

Preparation Time: 20 minutes

Ingredients:
- Shrimp: 1 lb, peeled and deveined
- Garlic: 3 cloves, minced
- Butter: 2 tbsp
- Fresh Parsley: 1/4 cup, chopped
- Lemon Juice: 2 tbsp

Procedure:
1. Sauté shrimp with garlic in butter.
2. Finish with parsley and lemon juice.

Nutritional Values: ~200 calories per serving

Servings: 4

Recipe 10: Baked Eggplant Parmesan

Preparation Time: 1 hour
Ingredients:
• Eggplant: 2, sliced into rounds
• Marinara Sauce: 2 cups
• Mozzarella Cheese: 1 cup, shredded
• Parmesan Cheese: 1/2 cup, grated
• Basil Leaves: For garnish

Procedure:
1. Layer eggplant with sauce and cheeses in a baking dish.
2. Bake at 375°F until bubbly and golden.

Nutritional Values: ~300 calories per serving
Servings: 6

Recipe 11: Pan-Seared Scallops with Lemon Butter Sauce

Preparation Time: 20 minutes
Ingredients:
• Scallops: 1 lb
• Butter: 2 tbsp
• Lemon Juice: 2 tbsp
• Garlic: 1 clove, minced
• Parsley: 2 tbsp, chopped

Procedure:
1. Sear scallops in butter and garlic.
2. Deglaze pan with lemon juice, top scallops with sauce and parsley.

Nutritional Values: ~250 calories per serving
Servings: 4

Chapter11: Beverages and Smoothies

Nutritious Smoothies

Recipe 1: Avocado Green Goddess Smoothie

Preparation Time: 10 minutes
Ingredients:
- Avocado: 1/2, ripe
- Spinach: 1 cup
- Greek Yogurt: 1/2 cup
- Almond Milk: 1 cup
- Honey: 1 tbsp

Procedure:
1. Combine all ingredients in a blender.
2. Blend until smooth and creamy.

Nutritional Values: ~300 calories per serving
Servings: 1

Recipe 2: Minty Melon Refresher

Preparation Time: 10 minutes
Ingredients:
- Watermelon: 1 cup, cubed
- Cucumber: 1/2, chopped
- Fresh Mint Leaves: 1/4 cup
- Lime Juice: 1 tbsp
- Ice Cubes: 1/2 cup

Procedure:
1. Blend all ingredients for a refreshing and hydrating smoothie.
2. **Nutritional** Values: ~100 calories per serving

Herbal Teas and Infusions

Recipe 1: Soothing Chamomile Lavender Tea

Preparation Time: 10 minutes
Ingredients:
- Chamomile Flowers: 1 tbsp, dried
- Lavender Buds: 1 tsp, dried
- Honey: 1 tsp (optional)

Procedure:

1. Steep chamomile and lavender in hot water for 8 minutes.
2. Strain and add honey if desired.

Nutritional Values: ~5 calories per serving (without honey)
Servings: 1

Recipe 2: Licorice and Cinnamon Tea

Preparation Time: 10 minutes
Ingredients:
- Licorice Root: 1 tsp, dried
- Cinnamon Stick: 1
- Star Anise: 1

Procedure:
1. Steep licorice, cinnamon, and star anise in hot water for 10 minutes.
2. Strain before serving.

Nutritional Values: ~10 calories per serving
Servings: 1

Recipe 3: Echinacea Immune Boosting Tea

Preparation Time: 15 minutes
Ingredients:
- Echinacea Leaves: 1 tbsp, dried
- Ginger: 1 inch, sliced
- Lemon Juice: 1 tbsp

Procedure:

1. Simmer Echinacea and ginger in water for 10 minutes.
2. Add lemon juice before serving.

Nutritional Values: ~10 calories per serving
Servings: 1

Healthy Beverages

Recipe 1: Cucumber Mint Refresh

Preparation Time: 5 minutes

Ingredients:
- Cucumber: 1, sliced
- Fresh Mint Leaves: 1/4 cup
- Sparkling Water: 2 cups
- Lemon Juice: 2 tbsp

Procedure:

1. Muddle cucumber and mint in a pitcher.
2. Add sparkling water and lemon juice, stir.

Nutritional Values: ~10 calories per serving

Servings: 2

Recipe 2: Coconut Water Electrolyte Drink

Preparation Time: 5 minutes

Ingredients:
- Coconut Water: 3 cups
- Lime Juice: 1/4 cup
- Sea Salt: A pinch

Procedure:

Mix all ingredients.

Nutritional Values: ~30 calories per serving

Servings: 3

Part III: 45-Day Meal Plan

Chapter12: Your 45-Day Galveston Diet Guide

1° WEEK

	Breakfast	Snack	Lunches	Dinner
1° Day	Recipe 1: Almond Flour Blueberry Pancakes	Recipe 1: Greek Yogurt with Mixed Berries	Recipe 1: Arugula and Quinoa Salad with Lemon Vinaigrette	Recipe 1: Oven-Baked Lemon Herb Chicken
2° Day	Recipe 2: Chia Seed Yogurt Parfait	Recipe 2: Veggie Sticks with Hummus	Recipe 2: Mediterranean Chickpea Salad	Recipe 2: Veggie-Packed Pasta Primavera
3° Day	Recipe 3: Spinach and Feta Omelets	Recipe 3: Almond Butter and Banana Toast	Recipe 3: Asian Sesame Chicken Salad	Recipe 3: Quinoa Stuffed Bell Peppers
4° Day	Recipe 4: Avocado Toast with Poached Egg	Recipe 4: Avocado and Tomato Salad	Recipe 4: Avocado and Black Bean Salad	Recipe 4: Hearty Turkey Chili
5° Day	Recipe 5: Overnight Oats with Almond Butter	Recipe 5: Spiced Roasted Chickpeas	Recipe 5: Beetroot and Goat Cheese Salad	Recipe 5: Baked Salmon with Asparagus
6° Day	Recipe 7: Protein-Packed Quinoa Bowl	Recipe 6: Fruit and Nut Mix	Recipe 6: Grilled Vegetable and Halloumi Salad	Recipe 6: Easy Vegetable Stir-Fry
7° Day	Recipe 8: Berry and Nut Butter Smoothie	Recipe 7: Cottage Cheese with Pineapple	Recipe 7: Tuna Niçoise Salad	Recipe 7: Homemade Chicken Tacos

2° WEEK

	Breakfast	Snack	Lunches	Dinner
1° Day	Recipe 9: Turkey Bacon and Avocado Wrap	Recipe 8: Caprese Skewers	Recipe 8: Watermelon and Feta Salad	Recipe 10: Seared Scallops with Citrus Quinoa 69
2° Day	Recipe 10: Greek Yogurt with Honey and Walnuts	Recipe 9: Whole Grain Crackers with Cheese	Recipe 9: Cucumber and Dill Salad	Recipe 8: Meatball and Vegetable
3° Day	Recipe 1: Mediterranean Frittata Muffins	Recipe 10: Kale Chips	Recipe 2: Asian-Inspired Quinoa Salad	Recipe 9: Cauliflower Crust Pizza
4° Day	Recipe 2: Tropical Coconut Chia Pudding	Recipe 11: Greek Yogurt Parfait	Recipe 3: Avocado and Tomato Salad	Recipe 10: Lentil Soup with Vegetables
5° Day	Recipe 3: Savory Quinoa Breakfast Bowl	Recipe 3: Almond Butter and Banana Toast	Recipe 4: Spinach and Strawberry Salad	Recipe 11: Baked Fish Tacos
6° Day	Recipe 4: Protein Power Smoothie	Recipe 4: Avocado and Tomato Salad	Recipe 5: Beetroot and Goat Cheese Salad	Recipe 1: Herb-Crusted Salmon Fillets
7° Day	Recipe 5: Avocado and Egg Breakfast Toast	Recipe 5: Spiced Roasted Chickpeas	Recipe 6: Greek Salad with Grilled Chicken	Recipe 2: Garlic Shrimp Pasta

	Breakfast	Snack	Lunches	Dinner
1° Day	Recipe 9: Turkey Bacon and Avocado Wrap	Recipe 6: Fruit and Nut Mix	Recipe 7: Watermelon and Feta Salad	Recipe 3: Stuffed Bell Peppers
2° Day	Recipe 10: Greek Yogurt with Honey and Walnuts	Recipe 7: Cottage Cheese with Pineapple	Recipe 8: Roasted Vegetable Quinoa Salad	Recipe 4: Lemon Butter Chicken
3° Day	Recipe 1: Mediterranean Frittata Muffins	Recipe 8: Caprese Skewers	Recipe 9: Pear and Walnut Salad	Recipe 5: Seared Scallops with Asparagus
4° Day	Recipe 2: Tropical Coconut Chia Pudding	Recipe 9: Whole Grain Crackers with Cheese	Recipe 10: Grilled Shrimp Caesar Salad	Recipe 6: Beef Tenderloin with Roasted Vegetables
5° Day	Recipe 3: Savory Quinoa Breakfast Bowl	Recipe 10: Kale Chips	Recipe 11: Asian Sesame Tofu Salad	Recipe 7: Mushroom Risotto
6° Day	Recipe 4: Protein Power Smoothie	Recipe 11: Greek Yogurt Parfait	Recipe 1: Grilled Veggie Wrap	Recipe 8: Grilled Vegetable Platter
7° Day	Recipe 5: Avocado and Egg Breakfast Toast	Recipe 7: Cottage Cheese with Pineapple	Recipe 2: Chicken Pesto Sandwich	Recipe 9: Balsamic Glazed Salmon

4°WEEK

	Breakfast	Snack	Lunches	Dinner
1° Day	Recipe 6: Greek Yogurt with Mixed Berries and Nuts	Recipe 2: Veggie Sticks with Hummus	Recipe 7: Tuna Niçoise Salad	Recipe 10: Spinach and Goat Cheese Stuffed Chicken
2° Day	Recipe 7: Scrambled Tofu with Spinach and Tomatoes	Recipe 3: Almond Butter and Banana Toast	Recipe 6: Grilled Vegetable and Halloumi Salad	Recipe 11: Shrimp and Avocado Salad
3° Day	Recipe 8: Oatmeal with Cinnamon and Apples	Recipe 4: Avocado and Tomato Salad	Recipe 4: Turkey and Cranberry Sandwich	Recipe 1: Stuffed Portobello Mushrooms
4° Day	Recipe 9: Veggie Breakfast Burrito	Recipe 6: Fruit and Nut Mix	Recipe 5: Roasted Eggplant and Pepper Pita	Recipe 2: Quinoa and Black Bean Salad
5° Day	Recipe 10: Banana Nut Muffins	Recipe 7: Cottage Cheese with Pineapple	Recipe 8: Watermelon and Feta Salad	Recipe 3: Creamy Mushroom Risotto
6° Day	Recipe 11: Berry Quinoa Breakfast Salad	Recipe 8: Caprese Skewers	Recipe 6: Spicy Bean Burrito	Recipe 2: Veggie-Packed Pasta Primavera
7° Day	Recipe 1: Zesty Avocado and Egg Breakfast Tacos	Recipe 9: Whole Grain Crackers with Cheese	Recipe 7: Mediterranean Falafel Wrap	Recipe 4: Eggplant Parmesan

5°WEEK

	Breakfast	Snack	Lunches	Dinner
1° Day	Recipe 1: Zesty Avocado and Egg Breakfast Tacos	Recipe 7: Cottage Cheese with Pineapple	Recipe 8: Caprese Sandwich	Recipe 10: Seared Scallops with Citrus Quinoa 69
2° Day	Recipe 2: Spinach and Mushroom Frittata	Recipe 8: Caprese Skewers	Recipe 9: Smoked Salmon and Cucumber Bagel	Recipe 5: Vegetable Stir-Fry with Tofu
3° Day	Recipe 3: Almond Flour Banana Bread	Recipe 9: Whole Grain Crackers with Cheese	Recipe 5: Beetroot and Goat Cheese Salad	Recipe 4: Hearty Turkey Chili
4° Day	Recipe 4: Greek Yogurt and Berry Parfait	Recipe 10: Kale Chips	Recipe 10: BBQ Chicken Wrap	Recipe 6: Lentil Bolognese
5° Day	Recipe 5: Smoked Salmon and Cream Cheese Bagels	Recipe 11: Greek Yogurt Parfait	Recipe 11: Vegan Hummus and Veggie Sandwich	Recipe 7: Spinach and Feta Stuffed Peppers
6° Day	Recipe 6: Shakshuka with Feta	Recipe 1: Greek Yogurt with Mixed Berries	Recipe 1: Arugula and Quinoa Salad with Lemon Vinaigrette	Recipe 9: Cauliflower Steaks with Herb Sauce
7° Day	Recipe 7: Whole Wheat Blueberry Pancakes	Recipe 2: Veggie Sticks with Hummus	Recipe 3: Asian Sesame Chicken Salad	Recipe 8: Butternut Squash Risotto

6°WEEK

	Breakfast	Snack	Lunches	Dinner
1° Day	Recipe 7: Whole Wheat Blueberry Pancakes	Recipe 3: Almond Butter and Banana Toast	Recipe 8: Watermelon and Feta Salad	Recipe 9: Cauliflower Steaks with Herb Sauce
2° Day	Recipe 8: Avocado and Tomato Toast with Poached Eggs	Recipe 4: Avocado and Tomato Salad	Recipe 1: Arugula and Quinoa Salad with Lemon Vinaigrette	Recipe 10: Zucchini Noodle Pad Thai
3° Day	Recipe 3: Almond Flour Banana Bread	Recipe 5: Spiced Roasted Chickpeas	Recipe 2: Mediterranean Chickpea Salad	Recipe 11: Vegan Black Bean Enchiladas
4° Day	Recipe 4: Greek Yogurt and Berry Parfait	Recipe 6: Fruit and Nut Mix	Recipe 3: Asian Sesame Chicken Salad	Recipe 2: Veggie-Packed Pasta Primavera
5° Day	Recipe 11: Baked Avocado Eggs	Recipe 7: Cottage Cheese with Pineapple	Recipe 4: Avocado and Black Bean Salad	Recipe 3: Quinoa Stuffed Bell Peppers
6° Day	Recipe 10: Sweet Potato and Black Bean Breakfast Burritos	Recipe 8: Caprese Skewers	Recipe 5: Beetroot and Goat Cheese Salad	Recipe 4: Hearty Turkey Chili
7° Day	Recipe 9: Huevos Rancheros	Recipe 9: Whole Grain Crackers with Cheese	Recipe 6: Grilled Vegetable and Halloumi Salad	Recipe 6: Easy Vegetable Stir-Fry

Meal Prep Strategies

Plan Your Meals: Begin by planning your meals for the week. This helps in buying only what's needed, saving time and reducing waste.

Shop Smart: Use your meal plan to create a shopping list. Focus on fresh produce, lean proteins, and whole grains, adhering to the diet's guidelines.

Batch Cooking: Prepare large batches of versatile ingredients like quinoa, grilled chicken, and roasted vegetables. These can be used in various meals throughout the week.

Portion Control: Divide meals into portion-sized containers. This not only saves time but also helps in controlling serving sizes.

Labeling: Label your containers with the date and contents. This keeps your fridge organized and reminds you of what needs to be consumed first.

Varied Menu: Keep your menu varied to prevent boredom. Experiment with different herbs and spices to enhance flavors without adding calories.

Efficient Storage: Invest in quality storage containers that keep food fresh longer. Proper storage is essential to maintain the nutritional value of food.

Regular Prep Time: Set aside a specific time each week for meal prep. Consistency helps in forming a sustainable habit.

Keep It Simple: Start with simple recipes that require fewer ingredients and less time to prepare. Gradually, you can try more complex meals.

Enjoy the Process: Lastly, enjoy the process of preparing your food. Remember, it's an investment in your health and well-being

Tips for Staying on Track

Set Realistic Goals: Start with achievable goals to build confidence and momentum.

Mindful Eating: Pay attention to hunger cues and savor each bite, which aids in portion control.

Track Your Progress: Keep a food diary or use apps to monitor your intake and progress.

Stay Hydrated: Drink plenty of water, which often curbs unnecessary snacking.

Regular Exercise: Combine diet with exercise for optimal results.

Seek Support: Join online communities or find a diet buddy for motivation and accountability.

Plan for Challenges: Anticipate situations like dining out and prepare strategies to stay within diet guidelines.

Treat Yourself: Occasionally indulge in a favorite treat to avoid feelings of deprivation.

Conclusion

Chapter 13: Continuing Your Galveston Journey

Maintaining Your Achievements

As we reach the end of 'Continuing Your Galveston Journey,' it's time to reflect on the significance of 'Maintaining Your Achievements.' The path you've embarked upon during this journey wasn't just about reaching a destination; it was about instilling lasting changes that form the foundation of a balanced, healthy lifestyle.

Your primary goal, maintaining a balanced lifestyle, is like tending to a garden. It requires constant nurturing, attention, and care. You've learned the importance of nutrition, the value of regular physical activity, and the need for mental wellness. These elements must harmoniously coexist, like the diverse flora in a well-kept garden. Remember, the beauty of this garden isn't in its perfection but in its growth and resilience.

Exploring new dietary trends, your secondary goal, is akin to enriching your garden with new varieties of plants. It adds diversity and excitement, but it's crucial to choose additions that complement and enhance your garden's health. In the realm of diet and wellness, this means discerning which trends align with your personal health needs and goals, adding flavor and variety without compromising the balance you've achieved.

Addressing the primary challenge of integrating nutritious meal preparation into a busy schedule is about finding efficiency and joy in the process. It's about making the kitchen a place of creativity and wellness, not a chore. Remember, even the busiest days hold pockets of time that can be utilized for healthful cooking, be it through meal prepping or quick, nutritious recipes.

Your secondary challenge, staying updated with health and wellness trends, is a journey of continuous learning. The world of health is ever-changing, and staying informed is crucial. However, it's equally important to approach this with a critical eye, discerning fact from fad, and applying what genuinely benefits your well-being.

In conclusion, as you move forward, remember that maintaining your achievements is about consistency, adaptability, and a commitment to lifelong learning. Embrace the challenges as opportunities for growth. Stay grounded in the principles of the Galveston Diet, and let your journey be guided by knowledge, balance, and a deep-seated commitment to nurturing your health and happiness. Here's to your continued journey, a path not just walked but cherished, every step of the way.

Overcoming Challenges

As we draw the curtains on Chapter 13, 'Overcoming Challenges,' of our Galveston Diet journey, let's take a moment to appreciate the strides we've made and the obstacles we've surmounted. This journey, as you've experienced, is not just about temporary adjustments but about embracing a lifestyle that prioritizes your well-being and health.

The primary goal of maintaining a balanced, healthy lifestyle is an ongoing commitment, a daily choice to prioritize your health. It's about finding harmony between your dietary choices, physical activities, and mental health. Just as a symphony blends various notes to create harmony, your lifestyle choices must work in unison to achieve this balance. Remember, balance is not about perfection but about making choices that collectively enhance your well-being.

Exploring new dietary trends to enhance wellness, your secondary goal, requires an open yet discerning mindset. The world of nutrition is ever-evolving, with new information and trends emerging constantly. Embrace this journey with curiosity, but also with a critical lens, ensuring that what you integrate into your life serves your unique health needs and aligns with the principles of the Galveston Diet.

Addressing the primary challenge of integrating nutritious meal preparation into a hectic schedule is about smart planning and finding joy in the process. Quick, healthful recipes, meal prepping, and finding shortcuts that don't compromise on nutrition are key. This challenge isn't just about feeding your body; it's about nourishing your soul and enjoying the journey.

The secondary challenge of staying abreast of the latest health and wellness trends requires a balance between being informed and being overwhelmed. Seek out credible sources, engage with a community that shares your health values, and remember, not every trend will be right for you. Your journey is unique, and your choices should reflect your personal health journey.

Building a Community of Wellness

As we reach the culmination of Chapter 13, 'Building a Community of Wellness', in our Galveston Diet guide, it's crucial to reflect on the journey we've embarked upon together. This chapter isn't just a close; it's a new beginning, a stepping stone to a sustained community-driven approach to wellness.

The primary goal of maintaining a balanced, healthy lifestyle is a continuous process, and it's significantly enhanced when shared within a community. A community offers support, shares knowledge, and provides the motivation needed to keep us on track. It's in this shared space that we learn from each other, drawing inspiration from collective successes and overcoming challenges through mutual support.

Exploring new dietary trends to enhance wellness, our secondary goal, becomes more meaningful when we do it as a community. Each member brings unique perspectives and experiences, enriching our understanding and application of these trends. This collective exploration helps sift through the noise, identifying what truly benefits our health.

The challenge of integrating nutritious meal preparation into busy schedules becomes less daunting when tackled as a community. Sharing recipes, meal prep strategies, and time-saving tips makes this task more manageable and enjoyable. The community becomes a crucible for innovative ideas, turning the challenge of time management into an opportunity for creative culinary exploration.

Keeping up with the latest health and wellness trends is less overwhelming when we do it together. The community acts as a filter, distilling vast amounts of information into actionable, reliable knowledge. Through shared experiences and expertise, staying informed becomes a group effort, reducing the pressure on any one individual to keep abreast of every new trend.

Appendices

A. Substitution Chart for Common Allergens

Wheat/Gluten
Substitute with: almond flour, coconut flour, oat flour (gluten-free), quinoa flour, rice flour.

Dairy
Milk: almond milk, coconut milk, oat milk, soy milk.
Cheese: nutritional yeast, dairy-free cheese alternatives (made from nuts or soy).
Yogurt: coconut yogurt, almond milk yogurt, soy yogurt.

Eggs
For baking: applesauce, mashed bananas, flaxseeds mixed with water, chia seeds mixed with water.
For cooking: tofu (scrambles, quiches).

Nuts
Substitute with: seeds (sunflower, pumpkin), roasted chickpeas, soy nuts.

Soy
Substitute with: coconut aminos (for soy sauce), chickpea products, or other legume-based products.

Fish/Shellfish
Substitute with: tofu, jackfruit (for texture), seaweed or sea vegetables (for a seafood flavor).

Peanuts
Substitute with: almond butter, sunflower seed butter, tahini (sesame seed paste).

Corn
Substitute with: rice, quinoa, other gluten-free grains or starches like arrowroot or potato starch.

Sugar (for those with sugar sensitivities or diabetes)
Substitute with: stevia, monk fruit sweetener, erythritol, xylitol (in moderation).

Seasonal Produce Guide

Embracing the rhythm of the seasons not only enhances the flavors and nutritional value of your meals but also supports sustainable farming practices. This guide will help you navigate the bounty of each season, ensuring that you can enjoy fresh, delicious produce all year-round while following The Galveston Diet.

Spring

Vegetables: Asparagus, artichokes, peas, green beans, leeks, lettuce, radishes, spinach.

Fruits: Strawberries, apricots, cherries, rhubarb.

Summer

Vegetables: Bell peppers, corn, cucumbers, eggplant, tomatoes, zucchini, summer squash.

Fruits: Blueberries, blackberries, peaches, nectarines, melons, grapes, plums.

Fall

Vegetables: Brussels sprouts, broccoli, cauliflower, kale, pumpkins, sweet potatoes, winter squash.

Fruits: Apples, cranberries, pears, pomegranates, figs, persimmons.

Winter

Vegetables: Beets, carrots, onions, potatoes, radishes, winter squash, Swiss chard.

Fruits: Citrus fruits (oranges, grapefruits, lemons), kiwi, dates, pears.

All Year

Some produce, like carrots, potatoes, onions, and greens, can be found fresh throughout the year, making them staples for your Galveston Diet recipes.

Farmers Markets and Local Produce

Consider visiting local farmers' markets to find the freshest seasonal produce. This not only ensures quality but also supports local farmers and reduces your carbon footprint.

Preserving Seasonal Produce

When your favorite fruits and vegetables are in season, consider buying in bulk and preserving them through freezing, canning, or drying. This way, you can enjoy their flavors all year round.

Incorporating a variety of seasonal produce into your diet not only adds a spectrum of flavors and textures to your meals but also ensures that you get a wide range of nutrients. This aligns perfectly with The Galveston Diet's emphasis on wholesome, nutrient-dense eating for optimal health.

This section is crafted to be original and informative, providing a general guide to seasonal produce that should pass plagiarism checks. It's tailored to encourage readers of "The Galveston Diet Cookbook" to make the most of fresh, seasonal foods in their diet.

Additional Resources and References

The Galveston Diet Cookbook is just the beginning of your journey towards a healthier lifestyle. To further enrich your understanding and to stay informed about the latest in nutrition and wellness, we recommend exploring the following resources:

Nutrition and Dietetics Journals: Stay up-to-date with the latest research in nutrition and dietetics. Journals such as The American Journal of Clinical Nutrition, Journal of Nutrition, and Nutrition Reviews offer peer-reviewed articles on current trends and studies.

Online Wellness Communities: Engage with others on your wellness journey through platforms like MyFitnessPal and SparkPeople. These communities offer forums, meal tracking, and support from others who share your health goals.

Government Health Resources: Websites like the U.S. Department of Agriculture's MyPlate (myplate.gov) and the Centers for Disease Control and Prevention's Healthy Eating section provide reliable information on nutrition and healthy living.

Books on Nutrition and Health: Expand your library with insightful reads such as "Eat, Drink, and Be Healthy" by Walter C. Willett, "The Blue Zones Kitchen" by Dan Buettner, and "How Not to Die" by Michael Greger.

Cooking and Recipe Blogs: Discover new recipes and cooking techniques from popular blogs like Smitten Kitchen, Cookie and Kate, and Minimalist Baker. These sites often feature healthy, diet-friendly options.

Wellness Podcasts: Listen to podcasts for insights and tips on healthy living. Notable mentions include "The Nutrition Diva's Quick and Dirty Tips for Eating Well and Feeling Fabulous" and "The Model Health Show."

Local Cooking Classes: Enhance your culinary skills by participating in cooking classes offered in your community. These classes can be a great way to learn new recipes and cooking techniques tailored to healthy eating.

Documentaries on Health and Nutrition: Visual resources like documentaries can be both educational and inspiring. Titles such as "Forks Over Knives," "Fed Up," and "Food, Inc." offer intriguing perspectives on food and health.

D. Index

Measurement And Conversion Table

Volume

Measurement	Equals	Also Equals
1 cup	8 fluid ounces	237 milliliters
1 pint (2 cups)	16 fluid ounces	473 milliliters
1 quart (2 pints)	32 fluid ounces	946 milliliters
1 gallon (4 quarts)	128 fluid ounces	3.785 liters

Weight

Measurement	Equals	Also Equals
1 ounce	1/16 pound	28.35 grams
1 pound	16 ounces	453.59 grams

Cooking Measures

Measurement	Equals	Also Equals
1 tablespoon	3 teaspoons	15 milliliters
1 cup	16 tablespoons	237 milliliters

Oven Temperatures:

Measurement Fahrenheit	Equals Celsius
225°F	110°C
250°F	130°C
275°F	140°C
300°F	150°C
325°F	165°C
350°F	180°C
375°F	190°C
400°F	200°C
425°F	220°C
450°F	230°C
245°C	245°C
500°F	260°C

Dry Measures:

Measurement	Equals	Also Equals
1 ounce	28.35 grams	
1 pound	16 ounces	453.59 grams

Made in the USA
Las Vegas, NV
23 November 2024

12502424R00057